Returning Home

Returning Home

Reconnecting with Our Childhoods

Jerry M. Burger

ROWMAN & LITTLEFIELD
Lanham • Boulder • New York • London

Published by Rowman & Littlefield
A wholly owned subsidiary of The Rowman & Littlefield Publishing Group, Inc.
4501 Forbes Boulevard, Suite 200, Lanham, Maryland 20706
www.rowman.com

Unit A, Whitacre Mews, 26-34 Stannary Street, London SE11 4AB

First paperback edition published 2017

British Library Cataloguing in Publication Information Available

Library of Congress Cataloging-in-Publication Data

The hardback edition of this book was previously cataloged by the Library of Congress as follows:

Burger, Jerry M.
Returning home : reconnecting with our childhoods / Jerry M. Burger.
p. cm.
Includes bibliographical references and index.
ISBN 978-1-4422-0680-9 (cloth : alk. paper) — ISBN 978-1-4422-0682-3 (electronic) — ISBN 978-1-4422-0681-6 (paperback)
1. Place attachment. 2. Dwellings—Psychological aspects. 3. Home—Psychological aspects. 4. Reminiscing. I. Title.
BF353.B87 2011
155.9'45—dc22

2010037474

∞™ The paper used in this publication meets the minimum requirements of American National Standard for Information Sciences—Permanence of Paper for Printed Library Materials, ANSI/NISO Z39.48-1992.

Printed in the United States of America

To my parents,
Richard and Mary Ann,
creators of my childhood home

Contents

Acknowledgments

I am extremely grateful to all the people who participated in the research reported in this book, especially the dozens of men and women we interviewed who disclosed so freely and so personally about their experiences. To protect their privacy, I have changed their names. But I've done my best to capture and retell their stories as accurately as possible. The interviews and their analysis would not have been possible without the hard work and dedication of my two research assistants, Linda Castro and Gia Vitarelli. Their contribution is deeply appreciated. Finally, thanks to the friends and colleagues who encouraged me to continue with this project. Many of their observations about places and homes are sprinkled throughout the book.

I years had been from home,
And now, before the door,
I dared not open, lest a face
I never saw before

Stare vacant into mine
And ask my business there.
My business—just a life I left,
Was such still dwelling there?

—Emily Dickinson

CHAPTER ONE

Returning Home

Three People, Three Stories

By all outward appearances and her own assessment, Laura was a happy and well-adjusted person. Her thirty-year marriage was strong; her three children had survived adolescence and college and were well on their way to establishing their own families. At age fifty-four, Laura could say her life had pretty much unfolded according to plan. She worked when she wanted, had always taken an active role in her church, and occasionally got involved in community events. There were no major health problems to complain about; no personal tragedies had altered her life. Then one day she found a box of old photographs in the back of a closet. As she sorted through the contents, she ran across a series of pictures from her childhood. One featured the large front porch where she and her family had spent many summer evenings. In another photo, she could just make out the old swing that once graced the background. As she flipped through the pictures, she saw the faces of her parents, siblings, and neighbors. Names she hadn't thought about in years popped into her head along with memories of achievements and embarrassing moments. For the next few weeks, images from the photographs repeatedly came to mind. Laura thought about the neighborhood she had grown up in, her favorite teachers from elementary school, and the view from her bedroom window. And as she thought about these people and places from her past, she sensed an emptiness she had never known before. It wasn't really homesickness, and it wasn't simply nostalgia. Slowly Laura recognized the problem. She no longer felt connected to the child in the old photos. She knew the smiling girl in the amusingly outdated clothes was her, but somehow the connection between who she had been and who she had become was missing.

Shortly after he turned forty-four, Brad felt a growing dissatisfaction with his life. His job had become boring and meaningless. He and his wife fought more often than they used to. Their youngest child had moved away earlier in the year, leaving the house quiet and empty. Too many evenings, Brad found himself staring mindlessly at the television, drinking more than he used to and feeling alone. Friends diagnosed his experience as "empty nest syndrome" or "typical male menopause," something they assured him would pass. But the feelings did not go away. Eventually Brad recognized that he had to make some significant changes in his life: his job, definitely; his relationship with his wife, perhaps. But just what he wanted to change to was not clear. He only knew for certain that he felt adrift, cut off from a basic foundation, without a sense of who he was or where he should be going.

Annie left home when she was seventeen and never looked back. Her alcoholic parents had never shown her much affection, but after her father died, Annie suffered unspeakable physical and mental abuse at the hands of her mother. When she was finally old enough, Annie left her small Midwestern town to attend college on the West Coast. She eventually began a career, married, divorced, remarried, and for twenty years did her best to erase her childhood from memory. Annie never tried to contact her mother and avoided speaking about her past as much as possible, even to her husbands. But her efforts to escape that past were never entirely successful. Images from those early years intruded into her passing thoughts and nighttime dreams. Annie suffered from bouts of depression she did not understand. As the years passed, she felt increasingly as if something was missing from her life. When her brother called one day to say that mother had died, Annie knew she could avoid her past no longer.

Although different in many ways, Laura, Brad, and Annie came to a similar conclusion about what they needed to do. In their own ways, all three decided they needed to get back in touch with something important. They wanted to reconnect with the people they had once been, with the values and lessons they had once learned, and, perhaps as a result, with who they had become. And so they decided on a similar course of action.

They all went home.

America on the Move

One out of seven people in this country changes addresses each year,[1] and fewer than ten out of a hundred live at the same address they did thirty years ago.[2] This mobility is especially prevalent among young adults as they move out of their parents' homes, go away to college, and take jobs in another city. People in southern and western states are more frequent movers than those back east. More than one out of five Nevada residents lived in a different home last year. But even in New York—the least mobile state in the country—one out of ten moves every year.[3]

These statistics tell us that few people remain in physical contact with the settings that made up their childhood experiences. The young couple that settles down in their hometown and remains in the same house, where the family gathers for the holidays and eventually grandchildren visit, is much more the exception than the rule. In fact, relatively few Americans even live in the same general area they grew up in. Most of us reside in different cities and often in different states. Increasingly, we live in different countries.

But while we may not live in the same place where we grew up, in most cases that place still exists. The house from our childhood probably still stands, even if someone else lives there now. Most likely, the schools are there too, as are the neighbor's homes, the woods, the parks, and the public swimming pool. I often hear people express the sentiment captured in the title of Thomas Wolfe's novel *You Can't Go Home Again*. If they mean by this that we can never become children again, that the world we once knew no longer exists, and that people and places change, they are correct. But if people use this expression to say there is no benefit to returning to a childhood home or that it is best to put the past behind us and focus only on the present, they are wrong.

Millions of people in this country have gone home again. They return to see the buildings and physical features that made up the landscape of their childhoods. Many make the trip alone, but quite a few bring along family members and loved ones. Some plan their trips for years, while others act on a whim. For more than a decade, I have surveyed and interviewed hundreds of people in an effort to better understand the experience of visiting a former home. Many of the stories I've collected are in this book. For some people the trip was joyful; others found it painful. A few were uncertain if the visit helped, but nearly all were glad they had made it. Most wanted to go back someday. But some said they had accomplished all they needed in one trip.

I'm not talking about visiting people from the past, although many of the individuals I interviewed did make time to see old friends and acquaintances. Rather, I'm interested in people who make trips specifically to see the places from their past. The individuals I spoke with wanted to visit the buildings, stores, playgrounds, and schools from their childhoods. In fact, many actively avoided running into people they once knew. Their quest was to connect with something only the place could provide.

Of course, the buildings people once lived in—their former homes—were always the focal point of their trips. Among the surprising discoveries for me was the large number of people who knocked on the door of a former home and asked the current owners if they could look around. Without exception, the visitors were invited inside. Imagine the reaction of the woman in Wichita, Kansas, who answered her door one day and found Jack Nicholson, Warren Beatty, and Annette Bening standing on her porch.[4] The three stars had a short layover during their cross-country flight, and Annette Bening thought it would be nice to visit the home she grew up in. The actors were invited inside and stayed forty-five minutes. Coincidentally, a few years later, Jack Nicholson played the role of Warren Schmidt, a recent retiree and widower, in the movie *About Schmidt*. As the character grapples with nagging questions about what he has accomplished in life, he decides to visit significant places from his past. Among his first stops is his childhood home, which he discovers is now the site of a tire shop.

Connecting with Our Past

The desire to stay in touch with our past is neither strange nor uncommon. In fact, most of us go about satisfying this need almost daily. Many people stay connected by listening to music that was popular when they were young. Where I live, I can tune in radio stations specializing in music from each of several decades. One station plays golden oldies from the 1950s and 1960s; two feature classic rock from the late 1960s and early 1970s. One station limits itself to songs recorded between 1970 and 1979, another to songs from the 1980s. Of course, we might like music from a specific period simply because we listened to a lot of radio in those days and became accustomed to a certain sound. But music also has a powerful ability to take us back to the era it represents.

Foods also connect us with our past. Homemade ice cream in the summer, freshly picked apples in the fall, and hot cocoa in the winter often trigger pleasant childhood memories. You may have found yourself purchasing a certain kind of candy or soft drink simply because you ran across it in a grocery store and hadn't tasted it in years. People also connect with their pasts by relying on recipes they learned from their parents or by packing lunches similar to the ones they enjoyed as children. I know one psychologist who tells her clients to try a dish of ice cream the next time they start to feel a little down. She finds ice cream often brings back feelings of security from a happier time.

Some people report a comparable experience when encountering certain kinds of weather. A summer rain can remind a transplanted Iowan of the

Midwestern storms she knew as a child. Snow, wind, thunder, and fog can have similar effects. I know a native Chicagoan who loves everything about her California home—with one exception. She misses the dramatic change of seasons, particularly the transition from summer to autumn. Each October she drives to the nearby Sierra Nevada mountains to experience the crisp morning air that tells her unmistakably that fall is on the way.

Rituals surrounding holidays and special occasions also provide avenues to our childhood. This is why newlyweds sometimes disagree over matters that seem trivial to an outsider. Her family always opens presents on Christmas Eve; his waits until Christmas morning. Her family sits down to a midday meal on Thanksgiving; his waits until evening. Photo albums and high school yearbooks also keep us connected with our past. Similarly, old home movies and, more recently, videotapes and DVDs provide a link with important times in our lives.

In a more formal way, reunions tie us to our past. Many people return every decade to see classmates from high school. Class reunions are said to keep friendships alive. But if that is the purpose, why do we wait so long between contacts? Perhaps it's the classmates we once knew whom we want to stay in touch with, not the aging adults who come together every ten years. Fraternities and sororities, military units, and even disaster survivors use reunions the same way. Members of these groups return to a significant time in their lives, a time too important to be relegated solely to memory.

In short, we do what we can to stay connected to the people and places from our past. But time is a relentless enemy of memory. Each year more details fade from our mental pictures. Friends move away. Sometimes they pass away. By the time they enter middle age, many people begin to feel that something is missing. As one woman told me, "I knew there was more to me than I could remember." Another woman described herself as "empty, incomplete, like there was something real important that wasn't there anymore." One man simply said, "It was time to fill in the gaps."

A Personal Journey

My interest in visits to childhood homes began with a personal experience. A year or two before my fortieth birthday, I noticed a nagging little feeling. At first it took the form of intrusive thoughts about my childhood. People and places I encountered reminded me of someone or some place from my past. As I drove to work, I found myself thinking about the local baseball park where I spent many summer evenings or the field behind my parents' house that, for all practical matters, was an extension of our backyard. I wondered about kids I had gone to school with and what had happened to some of my favorite teachers. Soon I was aware of a growing desire simply to go back and look at the places I was remembering. At first I tried to ignore the impulse. After all, my parents still lived in the house I grew up in and rarely had more than a year gone by when I hadn't visited. But as weeks passed, I knew that I wanted to return physically to the places that had comprised the backdrop for my childhood.

With a little urging from my wife, I made the trip. For three days I walked, bicycled, and drove around my hometown. I took a note pad and recorded whatever seemed relevant. I had written down beforehand some places I wanted to see and added to the list as I traveled around the community. The pool where I had taken my first swimming lesson was gone, and half of what was once my Little League diamond had been paved over. But otherwise, I was pleased to find almost everything on my list fairly intact.

Upon my return, I was certain the trip had been worthwhile, but I didn't really know how or why. That's when the scientist in me took over. Do other people have a similar urge to return to a former home, or is mine a unique experience? Is there a kind of place that calls people back? Is the trip a pleasant or unpleasant experience? Are people happy they went? And most important, if people make trips to places they once called home, why do they do it? I needed some data.

Surveys and Interviews

I began with a simple survey distributed to adults in several community organizations. After carefully working through the wording, I started the survey this way:

> Some people report that they have on occasion felt a strong need to return to a place from their past. Usually this means returning to the house they grew up in, but sometimes this also includes a desire to visit an old neighborhood or school. The places these people describe usually do not have any one specific memory associated with them, but rather are tied to a large number of memories. These also are not places the person visited once or twice in childhood, but rather are places that were part of the person's life for an extended period.

I asked people if they had ever felt a strong need to visit such a place (not just a passing inclination) and if they had actually made such a trip specifically to satisfy this need. If they had taken the trip, I asked them to describe the experience.

I was not prepared for the results. Excluding those whose descriptions did not match what I was looking for, 45 percent of the people I sampled reported that they had made such a trip. Another 18 percent said they had not actually visited their old home and neighborhood but had experienced the strong need I described. Obviously, I was not alone. Many people, at least among those in my Northern California sample, had gone through something similar to what I experienced. Moreover, many of their stories were fascinating, at times quite personal, and often touching.

Beyond the discovery that the experience is not uncommon, the most noteworthy finding in this initial investigation was the place people had chosen to visit. The vast majority identified a place they had lived in during childhood. More specifically, almost all had visited a home from their elementary school years, from about age five to twelve.

Naturally, this initial study led to additional surveys. I asked people from different parts of the country about this desire to visit a former home. But no matter whom I asked or how I phrased the questions, the findings were always the same. Visiting significant places from one's childhood is not at all unusual. Quite the contrary, it seems to be a fairly common experience. Coming up with an exact figure is a little difficult. Many people have driven through their old neighborhoods because they "happened to be in the area" or have seen their old homes when visiting parents still living there. However, based on several sources of data, I estimate that about one-third of American adults over the age of thirty have made a trip specifically to see the place where they spent their elementary school years.

I also learned that this desire to visit a place from one's past was something psychology had yet to discover. Hours and hours of searching through library indexes and dozens of conversations with other psychologists revealed that no one had ever studied—or was even aware of—this rather common experience. So I decided it was time to talk at length with people who had made such a trip. Perhaps by listening to them, I could better understand what this curious behavior was all about. The first wave of people I interviewed responded to the following 1" × 2" ad in the local newspaper:

RESEARCH SUBJECTS NEEDED

Santa Clara University psychologist would like to interview people who have ever made a trip to visit a place they once called home. $25 for a one-hour, on-campus interview.

My plan was to run the ad weekly until I found twenty or so people to interview. As it turned out, I only needed to place the ad once. My phone started ringing as soon as the morning paper hit the stands. Within two days, I had been contacted by more than a hundred people who wanted to talk about their experiences. After an initial phone conversation to screen out those who did not really match what I was looking for, I scheduled several weeks of interviews. Then my two research assistants and I went to work. The people we interviewed ranged in age from 21 to 79, with an average age of 49.7 years. Remarkably, exactly half of the participants in this first group were men, and half were women. Their occupations were quite varied. We interviewed a retired physician, a practicing minister, an author, and an unemployed homeless man. Some people had traveled to former homes as far away as Guam and Germany; others had traveled only a few miles. A few had returned home after being gone only a year. But it was not uncommon for people to wait thirty or forty years before making the trip. One man had moved away from Portland, Oregon, when he was eleven and did not return until he retired fifty-four years later. On average, our participants had allowed nearly eighteen years to elapse before something called them to return home.

Soon after I began the interviews, I realized I was tapping into a significant psychological phenomenon. Nearly everyone we spoke with expressed a great deal of emotion when talking about his or her former home and trip. Many smiled and described the joy and satisfaction they received from their visit. Some became sad, and a few expressed anger. Nearly one in five cried.

Several people refused the money they had been promised for their participation. Instead they thanked us for the opportunity to talk about their feelings and experiences. Many had believed the desire to see their old home and neighborhood was unique, perhaps even strange. Several said they hadn't told anyone else about their trip. They were relieved and reassured when I explained that they were far from alone.

I again saw the power of what I was investigating when I began to describe the research to friends and professional colleagues. Many had stories to tell of their own, and quite a few wanted to be participants in the research. When I present my work at professional conferences, I get more nods and questions than I have received for any other topic I've studied. The first time I talked about my research in one of my classes, one student burst into tears. She explained afterward that her grandparents were thinking of selling the house she grew up in, and she had not realized until that moment how emotionally tied she was to the place.

In most cases, the men and women I spoke with thought about their visit for a considerable period—sometimes years—before finally deciding to do it. Sometimes they packaged the trip with a class reunion or family gathering, but more often it was the place alone they wanted to see. What drew them to a place they hadn't seen in many years? What did they need? What did they hope to find? These were the questions I set out to answer. I began by asking about the place that came to mind when they thought about their home.

The Place We Call Home

Over the course of a lifetime, the average American will live in ten to twelve different houses, apartments, barracks, or dorm rooms. While some of these residences are temporary and forgettable, at least a few hold special memories. People often speak fondly of the first apartment they rented, the first home they shared with their spouse, or the house where their children took their first steps. But no matter how many miles or years removed, most people identify one place they consider their real home.

Where is that place? We asked the people we interviewed, Of all the places you have lived, which place do you consider your home? Some people wrestled with the question, but most had an immediate answer. All but a few identified the house or apartment they had lived in during their childhood as the place that came to mind when they thought of home. More specifically, it was the place they had called home during some or all of their elementary school years. Of course, it's not clear that we would have received the same answer if we had asked people who had never visited a childhood home. But, as in my initial investigations, the unique attachment people felt for their home during these early years was apparent.

In some ways, selecting a childhood residence as one's home is curious. Some participants had lived in that particular house or apartment only a year or two. In almost all cases, people had lived a far greater percentage of their lives in other locations, usually in another community. Some participants had not seen their childhood home in several decades before making the trip. Nonetheless, to them home was where they had grown up during these critical years.

But why these years? Many of our participants had an answer to this question. Quite a few talked about developing a sense of self during this time of life. In fact, more than a quarter of the people we spoke with mentioned "the formative years" before we did. More than a third used the interview to reflect on how childhood experiences shaped who they had become and what they'd done with their lives. As we'll see in later chapters, these individuals intuitively recognized what psychologists have discovered through research. The relationship between children and their physical world is indeed a special one.

The Experience

Just as no two childhoods are the same, no two stories people told us about visiting their childhood home were alike. Nonetheless, a few themes surfaced so often that my research assistants and I came to expect them. Of particular note were the powerful memories and emotions rekindled during the visit and the experience of comparing mental images from childhood with reality.

Memories and Emotions

Without exception, the people we interviewed talked about the flood of memories unleashed when they saw the old home, school, and playground. Typically these memories were not about dramatic events or turning points in their lives. Rather, standing in the middle of the road caused one man to recall the way neighborhood kids played baseball in the street between passing cars. Seeing a corner grocery store stirred up memories for one woman about a time she got in trouble for spending her lunch money on candy.

Visiting old elementary schools was particularly effective for reviving memories. Many of the people we interviewed managed to peek through a window of a former classroom. A few found open doors and were able to walk inside. In most cases, a torrent of memories followed. One man in his forties claimed he could recall not only exactly where he sat in his first-grade classroom but also the names and desk locations of every child in the room. Accurate or not, it's unlikely he could have recalled so many details without placing himself among the same closets, clocks, and chalkboards he had known decades earlier.

Smells and sounds also triggered memories. One man recalled backyard barbecues when he smelled the blossoms from a certain kind of tree he had not thought about in more than twenty years. Another woman responded to the sound of the surf smashing against the rocks where she had spent her childhood summers. Although she had visited many beaches in many parts of the world as an adult, her ears recognized the unique sounds of this particular beach. Memories of summers past followed.

Most of the people we spoke with also experienced a rush of emotions when surrounded by reminders of their childhoods. Many talked about feeling safe and secure. They remembered the comfort that came from being tucked in at night and the reassurance they found in their father's large lap. However, others recalled less pleasant memories. One woman cried for nearly the entire plane ride back after reliving some of the sad experiences from her childhood. Another woman described the anxiety that grew with each step as she moved up the walkway of her former home. In a few cases, the onslaught of emotions was more intense than the visitor had expected. One man found stepping into the old house overwhelming. He recalled taunting from playmates and the ridicule dished out by his mother. He had planned to stay in town for several days but left after two hours.

Similarities and Differences

Most of the people we interviewed started their trips anticipating clearly what they would find. Many used these expectations like templates, comparing the places they encountered with the places they thought they remembered. Not surprisingly, the most common discrepancy people reported was how much smaller everything had become. Slides that once rose threateningly high into the skies and playgrounds that seemed to go on forever somehow had become smaller and tamer. Enormously wide streets had narrowed, and immense lakes had become gentle ponds. The next-door neighbor's house was never this close. The walk to the grocery store certainly used to be longer.

Once these childhood perspectives were brought into line, many people found the places matched almost perfectly with their template images. "It was unbelievable, simply unbelievable how things had stayed the same," one woman exclaimed. "I could not get over how after all these years the picket fence, the trees, even the vines that used to grow up the side of the house looked like they had been frozen in time."

There is something very satisfying about finding places from childhood still intact. Our participants expressed particular delight when discovering some little detail that had remained the same. One woman was pleased to find the pattern of sidewalk cracks in front of her old home was exactly as she remembered. Another man found joy in discovering that the old path down the hill had the same turns and twists as before. One man we spoke with had waited forty-six years to return to his Hawaiian home. He found many similarities to the place he had left decades earlier, but best of all were the flowers he used to pick as a child growing in the same garden outside his former house.

However, most of the people we spoke with also discovered some differences between the place they remembered and the one they encountered. No doubt some of these differences were the result of imperfect memories. But others were due to the simple fact that places change over time. Our participants pointed out fences that had been erected, trees that had been chopped down, and buildings painted a different color. They also found that stores had change hands, neighborhoods had deteriorated, and empty lots had been developed. In almost all cases, our participants were not pleased to see the changes. Even those who acknowledged the improvements were at least mildly disturbed to find their childhood homes had not been perfectly preserved.

One woman was driving through her old neighborhood with her sister and discovered a "For Sale" sign in front of their childhood home. The women contacted a real estate agent and acted as if they were potential buyers. Although the pretense got them in the door, it also brought them heartache. They found a building they hardly recognized. Sometime in the preceding two decades, an owner had walled off sections of the spacious home to create a series of apartments. The beautiful backyard they remembered so fondly had been paved over for parking. Before walking through the door, the sisters had talked about using the same ruse to see other homes from their past. But after the initial experience, they decided not to risk further disappointment.

The Decision to Go

How does it begin? Why do people suddenly decide, after years of being away, that now is the time to go back to see the old home? We asked the people we interviewed this question. For many, the starting point was a growing preoccupation with childhood memories. Images from the past continually found their way into passing thoughts until one day they decided to make the trip. Other people pointed to a specific event that triggered their decision, such as running across an old yearbook or a memento from a special event. Sometimes contact with a former friend or family member set off a desire to return. One man decided to make the trip after his son drove through the old neighborhood on a business trip and reported back on what he had seen. A few people we spoke with just happened to pass by their former home when in the area for some other reason. A quick glance led to plans for a longer trip at some later date. For some people, the decision to visit a childhood home started with a current problem or issue in their life. As described in chapter 5, relationship problems or losing a job sometimes put people on the road to a former home.

Although most of the people we interviewed had planned their trips for a long while, others were surprisingly impulsive. Several people told us about packing a suitcase and jumping into the car almost as soon as they realized they wanted to go back home. The man who listened to his son's report about the old neighborhood had called the airline at once. Within a few hours, he was on a plane from California to New York. He had moved away from his former home twenty-five years earlier, and not until that moment had he ever considered returning.

On the other end of the spectrum, one participant's childhood home was also his place of birth. This man had developed an annual practice of returning to the house on his birthday at exactly 12:40 p.m., the time he was born. He never asks the current owners if he can go inside. Rather, he parks his car across the street and simply looks at the building and the surroundings. The house and the neighborhood have changed a little over the years, but not dramatically so. The man was sixty-six years old when we spoke with him, and he had been carrying on this same birthday ritual for years.

Three Primary Reasons

There are a dozen good arguments against making the trip. The traveling often requires a significant investment of time and money. And how do you explain to your spouse and family that you want to visit a Nebraska farm town or a New England village just to look at the buildings? Still, millions of people eventually get around to it. Why?

As with most psychological phenomena, the reasons people visit a childhood home are many and complex. But after I sifted through hundreds of stories, three primary reasons began to emerge. I would love to say that everyone I spoke with fit nicely into one of the three categories, but that is not the case. For some, the reasons for returning to a former home remained elusive. However, in most cases the decision seemed to reflect one of three motives. People visit childhood homes to establish a sense of connection with their past, to deal with current crises and concerns, and to work on issues from the past that won't go away. I'll describe the three motives briefly here and explore each in depth in later chapters.

A Place to Be

The most common reason people return to a childhood home is to establish a psychological link with their past and the person they once were. Although all of our participants, in one way or another, expressed a need to connect with their past, a large number identified this as the primary reason for their trip. Many of these individuals talked about their childhoods slipping away from them. Others felt it was simply time to renew memories about who they were and where they had come from. A few seemed to be going through a type of identity crisis. But most simply understood that there was something valuable to be gained from refreshing old memories or, as one woman put it, "keeping your childhood alive." Indeed, a few people told us that prior to the trip their memories were so vague and filled with so many holes that the images from their childhood seemed distant and unreal.

The desire to connect with the past sometimes extends across generations. Returning to a childhood home often revives memories of parents and grandparents, thereby strengthening a sense of connection with one's ancestors. Many of the people we spoke with took their spouses or children with them. They seemed to feel that by seeing the former home, school, and neighborhood, family members would be better able to understand the person who once lived and played in these locations.

A Place to Grow

The second most common reason for returning to a childhood home has to do with what's going on in the person's life at the time of the trip. Crises and moments of decision triggered some participants' visits. The issues they wrestled with included relationship problems, financial setbacks, and trouble with the law. Others said their visits were the result of a general need to reflect and reevaluate. These men and women wondered if their lives were shaping up the way they thought they would. One woman pondered whether she wanted to stay in her marriage. Another man came to see that his hard-driven quest to climb the corporate ladder had failed to produce the happiness and sense of accomplishment he had once anticipated.

To help them deal with these issues, these participants returned to the place where their values were established and immersed themselves in memories and emotions from crucial periods in their lives. Some visited the place where romance once blossomed. Others relived important moments by standing in the same location where an earlier conversation had taken place. In each case, these individuals were searching for information and insights to help them with the problems they faced in their current lives.

A Place to Heal

The third reason people return to a childhood home is to take care of unfinished business. Interviews with participants who fell into this category tended to be among the most emotional. Most of these people did not have happy childhoods. Many came from homes in which one or both parents had an alcohol problem. Many talked about emotional and physical abuse. Almost all had left their childhood home at an early age, hoping to leave their problems behind. However, as psychologists consistently find, deep emotional issues rarely go away on their own.

Some of the participants in this category visited the house where they had been victimized. Others imagined conversations they had avoided for decades. Some went to cemeteries and gave themselves permission to grieve for parents who had died too young. For most of these people, retrieving and facing unpleasant memories was but one step toward addressing issues they had been carrying around for years.

Catching Up to the Poets

In some ways, I am amazed that emotional attachment to homes has received so little attention from psychologists. Poets, novelists, and songwriters have known about the psychological significance of home for a long time. Henry David Thoreau reflected, "Only that traveling is good which reveals to me the value of home." Maya Angelou observed, "The ache for home lives in all of us." And Mark Twain maintained, "Our house was not unsentient matter—it had a heart and a soul, and eyes to see with." The treasured status of home is expressed each December by carolers who sing "There's No Place Like Home for the Holidays" and "I'll Be Home for Christmas." People who hear me talk about my research often mention movies and novels in which characters return to a childhood home. The list I've started already contains dozens of titles.

In short, it's past time for psychology to recognize the very real and often intense connection people feel with their homes. In the next chapter, I present the psychology behind this attachment. That chapter is followed by a discussion of the special way children relate to their homes. Then come three chapters devoted to each of the three primary reasons people visit childhood homes. Another chapter looks at the experiences of people who moved around so frequently as children that no single childhood home stands out for them. The last chapter ties the concepts covered in the book to some larger psychological issues.

CHAPTER TWO

A Theory of Home Attachment

I once asked a friend how she liked the house she and her husband had recently moved into. Because the new place was larger, newer, and better located than the house they had been renting, I was surprised by the lack of enthusiasm in her response. The house was fine, she said. Better than fine—really nice, actually. But clearly something was missing. After a short pause, she said, "I think Andrew and I just need to have a fight in every room."

Missing for my friend, I now know, was the emotional connection with her new house. In a sense, we develop relationships with our homes. And just as it takes time to form bonds with close friends and romantic partners, attachment to a home evolves as we invest time and emotions within its walls. My friend's new house was a nice place to live, but she needed to fight with her husband, decorate her Christmas tree, wallpaper her baby's room, and generally live her life in and around the building before the place felt like home.

In this chapter, I present the psychology behind the emotional connection people have with their homes, what I refer to as home attachment. Appreciating this connection is key to understanding why people visit places from their past and what they do when they get there.

What Do We Mean by Home?

Although we often use the words synonymously, many observers draw a distinction between a "house" and a "home."[1] In a psychological sense, a house becomes a home as we develop an emotional attachment to the place. Anywhere a person lives can become a home. People develop attachments to apartments, single-family dwellings, condominiums, boarding rooms, and dormitories. One woman I interviewed lived much of her childhood in a former army barracks. Another grew up in what had once been a chicken coop. Although their residences were unconventional and far from glamorous, both women had developed a strong emotional attachment to their childhood homes—a bond so powerful that it called them to return decades later.

People also use the words "home" and "family" synonymously. When we ask friends if they are "going home" for the holidays, we want to know if they're planning to visit their families, regardless of where those families now reside. People sometimes talk about going home when they reconnect with family members after an estrangement or a long period since last contact. This is what Robert Frost meant when he wrote, "Home is the place where, when you have to go there, they have to take you in."[2] However, when I asked research participants which place—of all the places they had lived—they considered their "true" home, the vast majority picked a location their family had long since moved away from. Nearly all thought of their true home as one they had lived in as a child. Thus, when I refer to home in this book, I mean the physical place, not the people who inhabit it.

Place Attachment

Among the most human of characteristics is our capacity to develop emotional bonds with others. Babies form attachments with their caregivers almost from the moment of birth, and we continue to develop and nurture emotional connections with the people closest to us throughout our lives.[3] When psychologists ask about sources of happiness, inevitably relationships with family and friends top the list.[4] But our capacity to develop emotional attachments is not limited to people. If pressed, most of us will admit to sentimental feelings toward a favorite hat, a worn-out baseball glove, pets, cars, an old uniform, or a stuffed animal we've had since childhood. All across the country, closets and attics are filled with items too outdated, too childish, or too worn to use—but too precious to get rid of.

People also develop emotional attachments to places.[5] Most obviously, we become attached to places where significant events occurred. Sometimes these are locations associated with one-time incidents. The bench in the park where you proposed marriage will always be special, as will the basketball court where you led your high school team to the league championship. However, like our attachments to people, emotional ties with places more often develop over an extended period. We form attachments to schools, dorm rooms, first apartments, summer camps, best friends' houses, the lake where we used to go fishing, and the place where we held our first job.

Of course, the place we are most likely to feel attached to is our home. Homes are almost always the place where we spend the largest part of our time, as well as the location for many of our most emotional experiences. People who visit their childhood home for the first time in many years typically find the trip an emotional experience. The feelings people associate with a former home, particularly a childhood home, are shaped by several psychological processes that make our relationship with the places we live unique.

Home Attachment

If I ever had doubts about the emotional bond people develop with their homes, those concerns evaporated soon after I started my research. The people I interviewed described intense joy when walking through former rooms and gardens. They delighted in discovering trees and playground equipment that had remained the same, and they talked about recapturing feelings of security and love that they had felt as a child. Others described painful memories and how they relived humiliations and regrets when seeing old classrooms and former friends' homes. A few mentioned the depression they experienced when finding the house was substantially renovated or, in a few cases, gone. Many broke into tears.

What can account for these emotional reactions? Like most things psychologists study, home attachment can be traced to a number of sources. Three in particular are worth a closer look. First, research over the past few decades demonstrates convincingly that our biological makeup often affects how we feel and act. We are the end product of an evolutionary history and, thus, should not be surprised that something as basic as a sense of home has roots in our biological heritage. Second, some of the attachment people feel for their childhood home reflects basic conditioning. In other words, we feel happy, sad, fearful, or content when encountering a former home because these were the emotions we often experienced when living there. Third, people develop emotional attachments to their former home because they often think of that home as an extension of their self-concept. Put another way, the places where we live become a part of who we are.

Biological Instincts

We cannot escape the fact that we are biological creatures. Evolutionary psychologists argue that much of what we consider "human nature" actually provides our species with a survival advantage.[6] For example, we are said to seek out social contact because the inherited tendency to live in groups helped our ancestors survive.[7] Similarly, one could argue that an inclination to establish and maintain a home base would have afforded our ancestors an evolutionary advantage. A permanent home location would have provided safety from predators and the dangerous side of Mother Nature. It also would have given families a place to gather and regroup, as well as a location for storing food.

To support their hypotheses, evolutionary psychologists often draw parallels between animal behavior and human characteristics. Images of salmon swimming upstream to lay their eggs and swallows coming back to Capistrano suggest that some notion of home is found in species other than Homo sapiens. In particular, animal researchers point to two behaviors often found in lower animals that resemble aspects of home attachment. These behaviors are known as home range and territoriality.

Home Range

Home range refers to the fairly confined area in which animals in the wild conduct their daily activities, such as hunting for food and searching for mates.[8] In other words, most animals don't simply wander freely. Rather, they identify an area that more or less encompasses their home space. Although researchers observe general tendencies within species, they also find each animal maps out its own specific home range. Cat owners often notice that their pet quickly establishes a circumscribed area in which to roam. I was surprised once to learn that my cat's home range extended much farther than I had ever imagined. A woman who stopped by one day recognized my cat as a frequent visitor to her neighborhood, which was more than a mile from my house. Home ranges can grow or shrink over time, sometimes vary with the season, and change with supplies of food and water.

Do humans also possess this tendency to establish a home range? Although it's easy to get carried away when pointing out similarities between animals and humans, a case can be made. Anthropologists describe what seems like home-range behavior when observing people in hunter-gatherer cultures, such as the Aka in central Africa and the !Kung in the Kalahari. One team of researchers looked at data from fifteen such cultures and found evidence for three kinds of travel ranges.[9] The smallest of these was the area typically traveled for the purpose of gathering food. A larger range included travel to visit friends and relatives. The largest range encompassed trips devoted to exploration and locating rare resources, including searches for mates.

When we pause to think about our own daily travel, most of us find we also limit our mobility to a fairly prescribed area. I once mapped out all the traveling I did for a month. I was surprised to see that the vast majority of my trips for shopping, entertainment, interacting with friends, and so on were limited to a relatively well-defined segment of the community I live in. With little difficulty, I could draw an odd geometric shape on a map of the San Francisco Bay Area that captured something like my personal home range. Similarly, a handful of researchers have borrowed the mapping techniques used by biologists to measure home ranges for children, teenagers, and adults.[10] These investigators find that people, like animals, typically limit their travels to an identifiable circumscribed area.

Territoriality

As animals compete for food, shelter, and mates, they sometimes "claim" and defend the resources within a certain physical area. Intruders are met with threatening gestures and, if they don't leave, with a fight. Biologists refer to this tendency as territoriality.[11] A single animal (typically the male) will claim a territory for itself and its mate and family, but herds of animals also show signs of protecting the group's territory. Animals rarely relinquish their territory willingly, and when they do, it is usually to a stronger and more powerful member of their own species.

As with home range, we can see a number of behaviors in humans that look like territoriality.[12] People often have places in their homes or at work that they think of as their own. Typically, these are spaces they control. Thus, a spouse may be asked to not disturb things in "*my* kitchen" or "*my* workroom." One study of Japanese housewives found that 84 percent identified at least one place in their homes that they felt they controlled, and 27 percent said there was a place in the home that was exclusively theirs.[13] Office workers also show signs of territoriality, sometimes even in areas not officially assigned to them.[14] Most people personalize their desks and offices with photographs, souvenirs, nameplates, and other individuating items. They arrange filing cabinets and plants to keep people from intruding too far into their area and become upset when someone uses their space without permission. Invasion of territory is a common complaint among administrative assistants who resent their supervisor's disrespect for their personal space.

Psychologists are often amazed at how quickly people act as if a space belongs to them, no matter how temporary the ownership. Within seconds, we start to feel as if we own this place in line, this seat in the theater, or this spot in the shade. One team of investigators timed how long it took drivers to back out of a parking space.[15] Drivers averaged thirty-two seconds to leave their space when no one was waiting. But it took them thirty-nine seconds to give up the spot when another driver was positioned to take their place. In a follow-up study, drivers took even longer to relinquish their parking place when the waiting car honked (nearly forty-three seconds). Presumably the honking was seen as a direct challenge to the parked driver's ownership of the spot. Finally, men (but not women) took less time to relinquish the parking space when the waiting car was a high-status vehicle, such as a new Lexus. This last finding relates back to the description of animals in the wild surrendering territory to more powerful members of their species.

As a university professor, I'm often amused by the possessiveness students feel toward classroom desks. As a rule, the desk you sit in the first day of class remains yours the rest of the term. When I schedule extra class activities attended by only a few students, everyone still finds his or her desk, even if this means sitting a considerable distance from others. A friend once passed along a piece of advice relevant to this point: pay attention to where you sleep the first time you spend the night with someone. If things work out, that will be your side of the bed for the duration of the relationship.

The Universality of Home

More evidence for a biological basis to home attachment can be found in the nearly universal tendency for people to establish a permanent home. Throughout recorded history, people in every part of the world have lived in relatively permanent locations. Upon close examination, even the few groups identified by their transient nature—the Roma people (gypsies) concentrated largely in Europe and the nomadic tribes in Saharan Africa—show the same general tendencies to settle into permanent locations as everyone else. The European gypsies' transient lifestyle can be traced to a number of factors that keep them from establishing permanent homes. These include the nature of seasonal work that requires migration, cultural practices, discrimination, and legal efforts throughout history to keep gypsies on the move.[16] In fact, when these factors are eased, the Roma people often demonstrate a desire to settle into permanent locations. As early as 1893, one census counted more than thirty-six thousand Roma people in Slovakia; yet, only 2 percent of these individuals were identified as nomadic.[17] Even when nomadic people move, they often arrange their new homes to resemble their former residences.[18]

Interpreting the Biological Evidence

So, what are we to make of the evolutionary argument? On the one hand, it's tempting to dismiss the parallels between animal and human behavior as interesting coincidences. Indeed, to argue that people protect their parking spaces for the same reasons lions protect their hunting grounds is to walk on thin scientific ice. Because it's easy to create a survival-of-the-fittest explanation for just about anything humans do, scientists often consider these observations weak evidence. For example, if people rarely developed an attachment to their homes, one could argue that constant movement provided our ancestors with a survival advantage by exposing them to new sources of food and places to hide from predators.

On the other hand, denying that biology plays any role in home attachment seems foolish. Moreover, acknowledging biological causes does not rule out the impact of psychological processes. For example, humans may have an inherited need to form relationships with other people, but who would suggest that social, cultural, and personality factors don't affect how these relationships develop? In short, rather than identifying biology as the cause of home attachment, we can say that it complements other causes. An innate desire to establish a sense of home is just a starting point. What interests me are the psychological processes that build on this general tendency and how these processes lead so many people to develop emotional ties with a place they once called home.

Memories and Associations

Perhaps the most obvious reason we develop an attachment to childhood homes is the same as the reason we form positive and negative feelings about any place: we had particularly good or bad times there. As anyone familiar with Ivan Pavlov and his dogs knows, pairing events and objects together leads to a conditioned association between the two. Just as the dogs associated a bell with food (and thus began salivating at the sound of the bell), a physical place can be associated with positive experiences, thus making us happy when we come into contact with it again.

Of course, the connection between our childhood home and the emotions it evokes is a bit more complicated than a simple bell-and-food pairing. Today, cognitive psychologists describe our memories as a vast network of connected images and thoughts, something like a series of nets or webs. Thoughts aren't scattered randomly around our memory banks. Rather, each piece of information is connected to related pieces of information so that recalling one memory makes it easier to think of related memories. That is why recalling the time your cocker spaniel fell into the swimming pool might cause you to remember the way your dog used to push his food dish along the floor when he was hungry, which may bring to mind a friend's dog that liked to eat eggplant, which might trigger images of the last time you and your friend went camping.

Emotions also get caught up in this web of memories and associations.[19] Spend a quiet moment thinking about a time when you felt especially happy, proud, or loved. Or, if you dare, think of a time when you were particularly sad, embarrassed, or lonely. If you are like most people, this exercise evokes at least a twinge of the same emotions you experienced when you won that scholarship or when you were the only person at that party without a date. Like sound that gets recorded along with the visual image in a movie, emotions are stored in memory along with information about our experiences. With time and effort, we can sometimes divorce the two, such as when looking back at a spilled coffee incident with amusement instead of reliving the original humiliation. But more often than not, it is difficult to separate the memory from the emotion.

If emotions and recalled images are linked in memory, then memories related to our childhood home most likely come with touches of joy, sadness, pride, and guilt. For most of us, our childhood home was the scene of many emotional experiences. Most of the key moments we spent with our parents probably happened within the walls of that home. Our childhood home also provided a place to spend time alone, to interact with friends, to grow close to or distant from siblings and other family members. Given what we know about memories and emotions, it would be difficult to not develop emotional ties with the place where all these events occurred.

Although all of us recall good and bad childhood experiences, I find that people overwhelmingly look back at their former homes with great fondness. One obvious explanation for these feelings is that most people had more positive than negative experiences while growing up. However, in all likelihood, our memories probably paint an unrealistically rosy picture of our childhoods. We have vivid memories of hitting home runs, but we don't seem to recall how often we struck out.

This tendency to remember past experiences as more pleasant than they actually were is a distinctly human characteristic.[20] Researchers find that, more often than not, we play down the unpleasant and boring parts of an event and exaggerate the happy moments. We forget about the mosquitoes on the camping trip, the awkward silences on the first date, and the pain during childbirth. But we recall with apparent clarity the celebration after graduation, the fun on the beach trip, and the warmth of caring friends. One team of psychologists asked a group of bicycle riders to report how they felt before, during, and after a three-week trip through California.[21] One week after the ride, the bicyclists remembered the experience as far more enjoyable than they had reported during the trip. During the bike ride, 61 percent said they were disappointed with the experience. Afterward, only 11 percent remembered that they had been disappointed.

Children are especially prone to seeing their experiences in a positive light. Shortly after my seven-year-old son played his first organized (sort of) basketball game, I asked him what skills he wanted to work on before the next game. He looked at me curiously and said, "I'm actually pretty good at everything." Given this self-assured view, we should not be surprised that memories from childhood are overwhelmingly positive. Because positive feelings toward childhood homes are probably exaggerated, the warm feelings we experience when thinking about the old place are likely stronger than a more accurate portrayal would allow. However, this fact makes these emotions no less real.

Home As an Extension of Self

Fond memories and biological tendencies can go only so far in explaining home attachment. Soon after I began talking with people about their visit to a childhood home, I realized the connection between people and places was much more fundamental than vague instincts or incidental pairings. As one woman I interviewed explained to her children, "If you know the places where I came from, you'll know me better." In short, places from our past are part of our self-concept. For most of us, the bedrooms, backyards, and classrooms that comprised the landscape of our childhood are part of our personal identity. To better appreciate this point, we need to look at what psychologists know about self-concept and the role other people and objects play in how we think and feel about ourselves.

Self-concept

Although each of us has a sense of who we are, we are not born with this knowledge. One of the many tasks newborns face is distinguishing the line between self and nonself. Infants soon develop a sense that the noise coming out of their mouths is under their control and that their hands and feet allow them to make things happen. Children as young as three months old react to a mirror in ways suggesting that they recognize that they control the reflected image.[22] One day my newborn son was sitting in his baby carrier making seemingly random—and loud—noises while my wife and I were trying to entertain guests. I apologized to my friends, adding that my son didn't usually act this way. One of our guests, a psychologist, found the whole scene—especially my reaction—amusing. "He's experimenting," she said. "He's trying to figure out what happens when he makes certain noises. Who knows? Maybe the television will come on, or maybe an elephant will appear."

The development of language hastens the process along. Variations of "me," "I," and the child's name are among the first words an infant learns. Then come nouns that identify objects and other people. Language provides the child with labels and thus the crude beginnings of mental categories to store information. Information about "me" is kept in a different category than information about "sister," although it will be a while before children fully appreciate that not everyone shares the knowledge they have accumulated. Among the early facts that enter a child's self-concept are the child's relationships with other people ("I am little brother"). By the time they are fifteen to twenty months old, most children have an understanding of gender and identify themselves as either a boy or a girl. They also develop an appreciation for age, recognizing that they belong to a category of people their own size.

Psychologists often describe self-concept in terms of cognitive categories. By way of analogy, cognitive categories are similar to computer files. They're the places in memory where people store the knowledge they have about a certain topic. We have separate cognitive categories for each of the important people, places, and things in our lives. Continuing the analogy, because information is stored in files rather that scattered randomly about our memory, once a file is accessed to retrieve one fact, other memories and facts stored in that same file are readily available.

Of course, the most important cognitive category is the one that contains information about you, what psychologists call your self-schema. But not everything in this category—that is, not everything you know about yourself—becomes part of your self-concept. To some people, dancing is but an occasional activity. But consider the woman who studies dancing and dreams of a career with a professional troupe. She would probably say that dancing is part of who she is, a part of her identity. Dancing is part of this woman's self-concept, but that's not the case for everyone who dances. Knowing the extent to which a behavior or characteristic is part of a person's self-concept helps psychologists predict behavior. For example, some people include daily exerciser as a part of their self-concept. That is, they think of exercising as part of their identity. Researchers find that these people are more likely to stick with a physical fitness program than those who think exercise is something they do but not part of who they are.[23]

Extending the Self-concept

Describing the self-concept inevitably leads to the question, Where is it located? At first blush, it seems obvious that the self-concept must reside in, or be limited to, what's inside the person—that is, our thoughts and memories. We might also include physical aspects of ourselves, such as our appearance, health, and physical abilities. But one's sense of self must end at the point where skin meets the rest of the world, right? This is, after all, the dividing line children learn when they separate "me" from everything else.

Although it seems intuitive that the self-concept is limited to what's inside the person, many psychologists argue that this view is too narrow. It's not that we confuse ourselves with inanimate objects and other people. But humans have a remarkable capacity to identify with people, places, and objects outside of themselves. Just as a professional dancer attaches her sense of who she is to dancing, each of us ties our identity to people and aspects of our environment that obviously are not part of our physical being.

The idea that individuals extend their sense of self to other people and objects is not new. In fact, we can trace this notion all the way back to the beginning of modern psychology. William James, the first acknowledged psychologist to address the question of the self, made this observation in 1892:

> *In its widest possible sense*, however, *a man's Me is the sum total of all that he* CAN *call his*, not only his body and his psychic powers, but his clothes and his house, his wife and children, his ancestors and friends, his reputation and works, his lands and horses, and yacht and bank account. All these things give him the same emotions. If they wax and prosper, he feels triumphant; if they dwindle and idle away, he feels cast down. (Emphasis in the original)[24]

Psychologists sometimes study self-concept by simply asking people to provide twenty answers to the question, Who am I? Not surprisingly, respondents typically describe the kind of person they believe themselves to be (an honest person, an extravert, a Christian).[25] About a third mention their gender, and many include their ethnicity and age. But people also describe themselves in terms of roles and their relationships with others (a teacher, a father). Most employed individuals list their job, just as nearly all married people and parents include their relationship with spouse and children when replying to the question. Among the consistent findings in this research is that women are more likely than men to describe themselves in terms of their relationships with others.[26] This difference probably reflects the frequently demonstrated tendency for women in our culture to place more importance on interpersonal relationships than do men.

In an interesting twist on the "Who am I?" procedure, one team of psychologists gave men and women cameras and told them to take, or have someone else take, twelve photographs that "describe who you are as you see yourself."[27] After coding the pictures the participants brought back, the researchers found relatively few photos of just the person alone. Out of 12 photographs, the men took an average of 4.2 of themselves alone, and the women averaged only 2.8. In fact, the participants included a large number of photos (4.5 for the men, 4.7 for the women) in which they themselves did not even appear. These photographs included images of family members and friends, but also pictures of pets, cars, motorcycles, alcoholic beverages, and a host of other nonhuman objects.

These and other studies suggest that people often extend their self-concept far beyond their own skin. For example, we commonly say that we are "proud" of family members when they achieve a noteworthy goal or act in laudable ways. But this pride makes no sense if we think of our self-concept in a limited way. If my wife receives an award for community service, what have I done to feel proud of? However, if we think of our self-concept as extending beyond our own thoughts and actions, then feeling proud when my wife does something meritorious is understandable. Because I tie my identity to her, it's almost as if I achieve something when she does. Similarly, most of us can think of times when we were proud of our children, our siblings, close friends, and even people who live in the same community that we do. Psychologists have examined this tendency to extend our sense of self in a number of areas. Let's briefly look at a few of these: romantic partners, families, social groups, and inanimate objects. Then I'll make the case that people also extend their sense of who they are to current and former homes.

Romantic Partners

Poets and songwriters often describe love as two people becoming one, as head-over-heels couples losing the line where one person ends and the other begins. Albeit less romantically, psychologists have also written about this you-are-part-of-me-and-I-am-part-of-you aspect of relationships. These researchers find that the cognitive categories we have for ourselves often overlap with those we have for our romantic partners.[28] That is, as you become romantically involved, the thoughts and images you keep in your "me" file become intertwined with the thoughts and images you have in your "partner" file. Soon it's hard to think of yourself without thinking of your partner, and vice versa. In short, your self-concept now includes this other person.

Demonstrating this cognitive fusion of self and partner requires psychologists to rely on some creative experimental procedures. For example, we know that people take longer to process inconsistent information than consistent information. The classic demonstration of this effect is known as the Stroop Test.[29] The test presents people with the names of colors—red, green, yellow—and asks the test taker to read each word as quickly as possible. The catch is that sometimes the word and the ink the word is printed in don't match. It takes people longer to recognize the word "blue" when it is written in red ink than when the letters are blue. Similarly, people quickly answer questions about themselves ("Are you competitive?") when they and their partner both possess the characteristic. However, these same individuals take longer to respond when asked about a characteristic that is typical of them but not typical of their romantic partner.[30] In short, people in love often process information about their romantic partner as if they were processing information about themselves. As the poets might say, two cognitive categories have become one.

Family

We also extend our self-concept to families and sometimes to specific family members. People often identify themselves as their father's son or their older sister's sibling. New parents frequently experience this metamorphosis in identity. Being "Jenna's mother" is suddenly central to a young mother's sense of who she is. The link between self-concept and family is especially strong for relatives of celebrities or members of famous families. In the United States, how could being a Kennedy or a Rockefeller not become part of your identity?

People from less well-known families also extend their sense of identity to their relatives, sometimes even to generations of people they have never met. Each year, tens of thousands of Americans attempt to trace their family trees. Dozens of organizations and online databases are now available to assist these searchers. But what's the appeal? Why is it important to know your great-great-grandfather's occupation and place of birth? When asked, family tree tracers tend to give similar reasons for learning about their ancestors. They want to know more about themselves. They want to know their roots, to get a better sense of their identity. Just as people are proud of their romantic partners and children, those who know their family history often point with pride to a distant relative who was a war hero or a former governor.

Social Groups

Human beings are natural joiners. Most of us belong to several formal and informal groups, from exclusive professional organizations to the regular gang that gathers each morning for coffee. Social groups serve a number of functions, but one often overlooked purpose of joining groups is that they provide us with a sense of what psychologists call social identity. That is, we often define ourselves in terms of the groups we belong to (in-groups) and those we do not (out-groups).[31] When answering the "Who am I?" question, research participants typically include group memberships (a fraternity brother, a band member, an American).[32] Just like romantic partners, sorority and fraternity members respond quickly when asked about characteristics they and their organization both possess. Yet, these individuals take significantly longer to respond when asked about characteristics that they possess but that do not describe their group.[33]

The tendency to identify with groups is powerful and perhaps automatic.[34] The way people instantly align themselves with others, even when simply assigned to a short-lived group, has long fascinated social psychologists.[35] Research participants randomly told they belong to Group X instead of Group Y almost immediately take on a them-versus-us style of thinking. Not surprisingly, long-term affiliations with groups we choose to join play a large role in our personal identity. For many people, being a member of the Methodist Church, a Southerner, or a Marine is central to who they are. An attack on the group is nothing less than a personal attack.

Inanimate Objects

If our identity can extend to other people and groups, what about something inanimate, like a car or clothing? Most of us accept that what a person drives or wears tells us something about the individual. But can we take this thinking one step further and say that a fancy car or flamboyant piece of jewelry is part of a person's self-concept? We all know people who hold onto a shirt or blouse so old and tattered that they would no longer consider wearing it. And people often speak of a "sentimental" attachment to a chipped coffee mug or an old piece of furniture. In many ancient cultures, personal possessions were buried with the deceased.

As these examples suggest, people often extend their self-concept to include inanimate objects.[36] This phenomenon is perhaps most obvious when individuals lose possessions they hold dear. People who lose personal objects to fires and floods often go through a process similar to grieving.[37] On the other hand, institutions that want to "depersonalize" new members, such as prisons and military boot camps, typically begin by taking away personal possessions.

Psychologists are often amazed at how easily people associate themselves with objects. In one study, participants rated a plastic cold drink insulator more favorably when they were told the item was theirs to keep.[38] When asked to evaluate the attractiveness of letters of the alphabet, most people show a noticeable preference for the first letter of their own name.[39] Psychologists refer to this last tendency as implicit egotism. Because most of us have a fairly positive view of ourselves, we are attracted to objects, people, and places that we associate with ourselves. Although associations with drink insulators and alphabet letters seem trivial and amusing, implicit egotism can also affect important life decisions, like career choices and where people live.[40] Researchers find that people named Dennis or Denise are more likely to become dentists than would be expected by chance. Similarly, people named Louis and Virginia reside disproportionally more often in St. Louis and Virginia Beach, respectively. This effect even extends to decisions about marriage. We are more likely to marry someone whose name resembles ours, even when that similarity is only the first letter of our last name.[41] Thus, Joseph will marry Josephine and Paula will marry Paul more often than chance would dictate.

Self-concept and Home

In short, ample evidence suggests that people often think of themselves in ways that extend beyond their own thoughts, emotions, and actions. It's not much of a leap, therefore, to suggest that we also extend our self-concept to places.[42] Consider the results of one investigation in which participants were given a list of ninety-six items.[43] The list included people (your mother), body parts (your hands), places (your neighborhood), objects (your favorite car), and other "self" concepts (your childhood memories). Participants placed each item into one of four categories, depending on how much they considered the object to be a part of their personal identity: self, a little self, a little not self, and not self. The researcher assigned a value of four to one for each item, depending on the participants' answers, and calculated the average ratings.

Not surprisingly, concepts we traditionally associate with self-concept—our values, our feelings—topped the list. Consistent with past research, special people in the participants' lives were also rated quite high. Mother, spouse, and father all fell among the top items on the list, as did some body parts, like eyes and hair. But also high on the list (at number 25) was current dwelling. In other words, most participants saw the place they currently lived as an important part of their identity. In fact, they rated their current residence as more a part of their self than their ancestors, the last school they attended, or religion. Another item, favorite room at home, also finished high on the list.

Do people really think of their homes and other important places as part of their self-concept? Back to William James, the nineteenth-century psychologist who recognized that people extend their sense of self beyond their own thoughts and emotions: "Our home . . . its scenes are part of our life: its aspects awaken the tenderest feelings of affection; and we do not easily forgive the stranger who, in visiting it, finds fault with its arrangements or treats it with contempt."[44]

Consider the similarities between the way we share personal information with others and the way we share our homes. Decades of research finds that people reveal information about themselves in a selective manner.[45] Personal details about dreams, hopes, and fears are limited to those we like and trust. In a similar way, we are selective about how and with whom we share our home. Passing through the entryway into another person's residence is not a trivial act. Etiquette demands that we do not step through a front door until we are invited in. One's home, like personal facts and feelings, is revealed at the owner's discretion. Indeed, it is a powerful statement when we say someone is "no longer welcome in my home." For the same reason, failure to share one's home can send an unfriendly message. I heard my father-in-law once question the depth of his friendship with a man he had known for years. "He has never invited me to his home," my father-in-law explained. "Not even once."

We see this same sense of protectiveness when people's homes are burglarized.[46] Burglary victims often report that they feel "violated" and that the image of an unknown and uninvited person walking around their home is more unsettling than the monetary loss from the theft. Some say it's like having their diary read by a stranger. In one study, more than half the burglary victims interviewed mentioned without prompting that they felt as if they had been "violated, polluted or raped."[47] This sense of personal invasion can linger for months.[48]

The connection between self-concept and home can be especially strong when combined with a sense of belonging to a community. During the Middle Ages in Europe, the link between identity and community was so prominent that names were often based on where one lived.[49] Thus, an Englishman might be known as William of Orange, and a French lady would be Mademoiselle de Chartres. Although it's less common in the United States than in other countries, many people develop an attachment to a specific town or geographic region. The bond is particularly strong when several generations have lived in the community. People frequently select a cemetery in their family community as the place they want to be buried, even if they themselves have not lived in that area in decades.

Consider the citizens of Princeville, North Carolina, as described by journalist Jake Halpern.[50] Halpern investigated people who continue to live in communities despite overwhelmingly good reasons to leave, such as the Hawaiian who refused to move even though his home was surrounded by rivers of flowing lava. Princeville is a small, rural town that some historians identify as the first incorporated township founded exclusively by African Americans. Many residents trace their roots back to ancestors who settled in the region after the Civil War. Unfortunately, the town is located on a flood plain and has a history of disastrous flooding. Nonetheless, Princeville held its own against Mother Nature until September 1999, when Hurricane Floyd bloated the river and for all intents and purposes wiped out the town. The Federal Emergency Management Agency (FEMA) studied the situation and made the residents an offer. They could repair the broken dike, rebuild their homes, and take their chances on the flood plain, or FEMA would bulldoze the remaining structures and give residents a cash buyout so they could relocate elsewhere.

A rational weighing of the pros and cons would certainly tilt toward the buyout and relocation option. But the residents' attachment to their homes—and the homes of their parents and grandparents—was strong. Thad Knight, a seventy-two-year-old resident who wanted to stay, escorted Halpern through the Princeville cemetery: "Thad and I stopped at a series of modest tombstones that all read, 'Knight.' Thad showed me the graves of his mother and father, and then he walked over to the graves of his three deceased brothers. 'This one lived in New Jersey, this one lived in Jamaica, New York, and this one was in Greensboro,' he said. 'They all wanted to be brought home.'"[51]

In the end, the Princeville town commission voted with their hearts rather than their heads. They turned down the buyout. The displaced citizens returned to Princeville and rebuilt.

It's easy to look at the Princeville residents' decision and scratch your head. I see the same reaction when people comment on communities damaged by fires, hurricanes, or earthquakes. People in California can't understand why residents in "tornado alley" in Oklahoma and Kansas stay in the same targeted town despite recurring tornadoes. Midwesterners who have lived through their share of tornado warnings don't understand why people who lose their homes and possessions to a forest fire return to rebuild on the same spot. People living in small forested mountain towns would never consider moving to a hurricane zone like Florida. And citizens of Florida read about earthquakes and wonder why Californians continue to sit on a geological time bomb.

Although disasters cause some people to relocate for good, in almost all cases the vast majority of a damaged community's residents return. Those who choose to move on are likely to be recent immigrants, renters, or other transient groups who have yet to establish roots in the community.[52] This appears to have been the pattern when Hurricane Katrina and the ensuing flood devastated the city of New Orleans and other communities along the coast of the Gulf of Mexico in 2005. Although a substantial percentage of the population left for good, the majority of the city's population returned.[53] Of course, financial reasons, such as property ownership and employment opportunities, bring people back or cause them to move on. But we should not underestimate the powerful draw of the emotional attachment people feel to their homes and communities.

Is Home Attachment Universal?

When I give talks about my research to groups of students and professors, I typically get three kinds of reactions. First, a number of people are visibly touched emotionally when I talk about attachment to homes. Many audience members nod when I tell stories of participants who visited their childhood homes. A lot of these people stop by after the talk to share their own experiences. Second, many people relate to what I'm saying but without the outward emotional response. Quite a few have made their own trip to see the buildings from their childhood. Others have not yet made the trip but have experienced the urge to do so.

But there is also a third group. Between a quarter and a third of the people in the audience have a difficult time with the whole notion of home attachment. They sometimes look with furrowed brows at those who talk emotionally about former homes. It's just a building, they sometimes tell me. What's the point of going back to see how much the place has deteriorated? I don't try to argue with these people. Their feelings and perceptions are as genuine as those who understand what I'm saying. But their reaction does raise some important questions. How universal is home attachment? And why do some people develop a strong attachment to former homes, whereas others see only wood, bricks, and paint?

I have three responses to these questions. First, the capacity for home attachment can be universal even if it is not expressed by everyone. As mentioned earlier, psychologists agree that there is a universal need for social contact. Yet, many people tend to keep to themselves, and it is not uncommon for people to seek out extended periods of isolation.[54] In the same way, it's possible that each of us has the capacity to connect emotionally with our home, but whether this connection is established and how it is expressed probably varies from person to person.

Second, some people simply may not have had an opportunity to develop an attachment to their childhood home. Children who move frequently during their elementary school years might not stay in one place long enough to establish an emotional connection. This is often the experience of "military brats," whose family is stationed in a new area every few years. I'll have more to say about these individuals in chapter 7. It also is the case that childhood memories are not always pleasant for those who stay in one place. The sad fact is that more than 3 million children in this country are referred to state and local child-protective services each year.[55] Children growing up in abusive situations are unlikely to develop a positive emotional bond to their former home. Nonetheless, as described in chapter 6, some people visit childhood homes specifically to deal with painful memories.

Third, to state the obvious, people are different. Although, to date, little work has been done on this question, how people relate to their homes may depend on personality differences. In one study, adults prone to emotional reactions were more likely to become depressed both before and after moving than those who were less emotional.[56] In contrast, extraverted individuals felt better about themselves after moving. Are there also personality differences between people who become emotionally attached to a childhood home and those who don't? To find out, I gave a series of personality tests to people who had visited a childhood home and to a group of individuals who expressed no interest in taking such a trip. I found significant differences between the two groups on five of six personality scales. People who had visited a childhood home had a stronger need to understand their own behavior than did the nonvisitors. The visitors also expressed a stronger need to seek out novel experiences, as well as a stronger need to act independently of social expectations. In addition, those who had made the trip had a greater interest in artistic and intellectual concepts and were comfortable thinking in unconventional ways. Interestingly, the visitors also scored higher than the nonvisitors on a measure of need for achievement.

Although these findings tend to paint those who visit childhood homes in a better light than those who do not, I caution against making any overarching statements about the two groups. I also asked these individuals to complete several measures of personal adjustment and found no differences between the groups on any of the scales. Thus, although visitors and nonvisitors may have different personalities, neither appears to be better or worse off emotionally than the other.

CHAPTER THREE

A Child's World

One day, when my son was about eleven years old, he and I had a conversation about our neighborhood. We had moved into our house when Adam was seven. It was in a typical suburban community—blocks of single-family homes, sidewalks, front lawns, a nearby park. During the time we lived there, I had visited neighbors, taken evening walks, and played with Adam in the park. From my perspective, I had gotten to know the neighborhood pretty well. This particular conversation was prompted by my son's story about how he and a friend had helped a neighbor locate her lost dog. As Adam provided the details of the search, I found myself interrupting at several points for clarification. Adam referred to "those rosebushes with the really big red flowers," and I had to ask exactly what roses he was talking about. My son described a passageway through the hedges that ran between two houses, and I asked which houses and what kind of passageway? Adam explained how he and his friend climbed the tree with the long needles and low-lying limbs to get a good view of the entire park. Where exactly was this tree, I asked?

It soon became evident that my son knew our neighborhood in a way that I did not. I knew the streets, many of the residents, and a few obvious landmarks. I also had a pretty good idea of which neighbors kept their yards mowed regularly and who had recently purchased a new car. But I knew virtually nothing about holes in fences, hiding places near the tennis courts, and which were the good climbing trees.

I know now that the different way Adam and I understood our neighborhood was not simply a matter of paying attention. Rather, a small but growing amount of research suggests that children do not interact with their physical worlds they way adults do. We may have walked together through the same landscape, but my son and I experienced the streets, lawns, and sidewalks very differently. However, ask me about the trees, sticker patches, and cracks in the sidewalk in the neighborhood I grew up in, and I'll give you detailed descriptions.

Why the Elementary School Years?

Among the unexpected discoveries in my research was the special bond people feel for the place they lived during their elementary school years, approximately age five to twelve. Few people visit homes they lived in prior to this age. And the ones who do are often more interested in seeing where their parents or older siblings lived than in learning something about themselves. Of course, people also form attachments with homes from teenage and adult years. But I found repeatedly that when people feel a strong desire to visit a former residence, it's most often the home from those elementary school years that they seek out. Why?

There are two reasons for this preference. The first has to do with a well-known psychological phenomenon called childhood amnesia. The second reason adults prefer to visit homes from their elementary school years is much less researched. Some psychologists speculate that children interact with the physical world in a unique fashion. Children don't simply make their way through the landscape. Rather, the buildings, parks, woods, and schoolyards represent opportunities to explore, manipulate, and create. More important, this exploratory and manipulative behavior may play an major role in developing a child's sense of individuality and personal mastery.

Childhood Amnesia

If I asked you to recall your earliest memory, you might be able to generate a few hazy images from preschool days. But if you are like most people, you probably recall little if anything that happened before age five. Psychologists call this inability to remember events from those early years childhood amnesia. Researchers set the absolute lower limit for any kind of memories at two years old. Yet even in these rare cases, the images are vague and often of questionable accuracy. People who claim to have vivid memories from when they were two or three are most likely recalling a photograph, an oft-told family story, or an imagined scene from these early years.

Although developmental psychologists continue to investigate and debate the causes of childhood amnesia, current explanations point to limits in the memory skills of toddlers.[1] The infant's ability to pull information in and out of memory is not very efficient. Preschool children record less information, forget information more quickly, and need more specific cues to recall information than do older children. The net result is that, while children learn all kinds of things about the world at an amazingly rapid pace during the first few years of life, their ability to recall specific events is minimal. Little wonder that, years later, none of us can retrieve images from our first birthday party or when we learned to walk. If those images were ever encoded, they were forgotten long ago.

In addition to toddlers' limited memory skills, recalling significant events from preschool years is hampered by underdeveloped cognitive structures. As described in the previous chapter, information is not stored randomly within our memories. Rather, facts and images are filed away in cognitive categories. Among the most important of these categories is the one we use for storing information about ourselves. For adults, memories stored in the self category are typically easier to recall than memories stored elsewhere. But remember that babies aren't born with a sense of self. Although pinpointing the moment a child develops this critical cognitive category is not yet possible, indications from several sources suggest that it happens around the end of the second year of life.[2] It is about this time that children start to use the words "I," "me," and "mine."[3]

Developing a cognitive category for self allows children to store and retrieve information about "me" readily. By the time toddlers are two and a half to three years old, they can accurately answer questions about important events (e.g., an emergency room visit or a trip to Disneyland) that happened several months earlier.[4] However, the child's cognitive system is still crude at this time, and memory skills are still developing. Researchers generally have to prompt three-year-olds with descriptions of the event and often have to settle for yes or no answers. But as children advance through the preschool years and into the first few years of elementary school, their memory skills improve, and their network of cognitive categories becomes more elaborate and efficient. As a result, most of us recall few or no memories from when we were three, some memories from when we were five, and quite a few memories from when we were seven.

Research on toddler's memories and childhood amnesia helps us understand why people don't often visit homes they lived in before the age of five. First, most of us have few if any memories about homes and neighborhoods from those early years. Thus, there are no memories to bring forth and no emotions to elicit by visiting the place. Second, as I argued in the previous chapter, people often view their homes as an extension of their self-concept.

In cognitive psychology terms, the thoughts and images we store in memory about our home are connected to, or embedded within, our self-schema. But if our self-concept was still in the early stages of development during the preschool years, the sense of self we have as an adult is unlikely to be tied to a home lived in during that time. Visiting a home from preschool years will probably do little to help someone who wants to reconnect with the person they once were.

A Child's Unique Relationship with the Physical World

When trying to understand how children interact with the world, it seems once again that the poets, novelists, and filmmakers are way ahead of the psychologists. We've all read stories or seen movies that express the wonder with which children encounter flowers and insects and the joy they find in exploring a riverbank or building a tree house. Yet, to date only a handful of psychologists have considered the way children interact with their physical environment. Although research is relatively sparse, a case can be made that children in their preteen years experience their worlds in a unique way. Perhaps the first to describe this phenomenon was Edith Cobb.[5] After studying children for many years, she drew this conclusion in 1959:

> There is a special period, the little-understood, prepubertal, halcyon, middle age of childhood—approximately from five or six to eleven or twelve . . . when the natural world is experienced in some highly evocative way. . . . Using various forms of so-called projective methods and play techniques. . . . I became acutely aware that what a child wanted to do most of all was to make a world in which to find a place to discover a self.[6]

Cobb argued that children's sense of individuality and mastery is developed as they interact and shape the physical world in their own unique way. She also proposed that creative adults, such as artists and inventors, often "return in memory" to these early days to recapture a sense of uniqueness and spontaneity. She did not mean that these creative adults literally return to their childhood homes to find inspiration. However, as I explore in the next chapter, that might not be bad advice.

Cobb and others observed that preteen children do not simply move through their worlds. Rather, they explore and manipulate the environment. They dig in the dirt, climb the trees, and follow the trails they encounter. This style of interacting with the world reflects two complementary needs. First, children need to establish a sense of identity apart from their family and parents. Children want and need a secure home and loving family, but they also need to develop a sense of who they are separate from the identity imposed by the family. This requires making their own decisions and—sometimes literally—creating their own physical place in the world. Second, children need to develop a sense of personal control or mastery over the environment. Well-functioning adults believe they can control, or at least influence, most of the challenges and demands life throws their way.[7] It's during these elementary school years, when they're able to perform more activities outside of parental supervision, that children come to see that they too can make their mark on the world. So they dig, and they build, and they climb.

And they explore. Roger Hart, an early researcher in this area, examined the distances children travel from their homes. He found a significant increase in these distances when the child reached age eight.[8] The typical child's home range expands throughout the elementary school years to include friends' homes, playgrounds, parks, stores that sell candy and ice cream, and just about any place on the routes in between. Not coincidentally, also about this time children develop the ability to make and read maps.[9]

It's worth noting that Hart's research was conducted in Wilmington, Vermont, back in the 1970s, a time when most children walked or rode their bicycles to school. Today, largely due to safety concerns, fewer than one in three children walks or bikes to school, and most eight-year-olds are rarely allowed as much freedom to travel without parental supervision as the children Hart studied.[10] Although these restrictions no doubt have limited some of the wandering found in earlier generations of children, the needs to explore and to manipulate remain. One of the ways children express these needs is through the creation of special places.

Special Places

If my memory is correct, I spent a good deal of my childhood in the large (or so it seemed at the time) field behind my parents' house. Our backyard gate opened onto an undeveloped plot of land that contained two radio transmission towers and a host of exploration possibilities. The wild grass was high enough to hide in during the spring. And there were remnants of water troughs and fence posts from an earlier farm, not to mention endless buried treasures. The kids in the neighborhood made pathways and makeshift play areas, but I remember the summer forts most. These were nothing more than holes we dug, rarely more than a couple of feet deep, that became the site of childhood adventures. Most of the summer, you could find three or four of these forts scattered about the field, each belonging to a different group of boys (for some reason, this was a gender-specific activity). Two or three boys would spend most of a day digging the fort, which then "belonged" to them until the radio station that owned the property plowed the field, which they did a couple of times each year. We played in these forts, hung out there, sometimes ate there. We gave them names. Uninvited guests were not welcome, and grown-ups were never allowed inside.

Later conversations with friends informed me that I was hardly unique in creating my special kids-only fort. As it turns out, a lot of people I know had their own private places as kids. For some, it was a tree house; for others, a secluded corner of the basement or a hidden place in the woods between trees and rocks. Some of my friends went to their special place alone; others shared it with a few close friends or a sibling. Often their parents didn't even know the place existed (or so they thought). But in all cases, parents most definitely did not go inside. And always, as far as anyone could remember, this special place was a part of their lives only during the elementary school years.

Do most children find or create places like my summer forts? To find out, I distributed a survey to a large number of adults. I began by explaining that children sometimes "identify places in and around their homes that are special to them." I also provided a few examples of what I meant (an attic, a tree house). I asked my participants if they could think of such a place and, if so, to describe it briefly. Although everyone wrote something, many of these special places were fairly general (my neighborhood, summer camp) or were more public than private (my school, the baseball diamond at the park). More specific instructions might have yielded different responses, but I wanted to see if people would recall the kind of private place I had in mind without much prompting.

In fact, most of them did. Of the participants in the study, 72 percent described the kind of personal, kids-only place I was looking for. About two-thirds of these special places were located outdoors. These included an old barn, a clearing in the woods, "an underground fort" (I especially liked that one), tree houses, "a place at the end of an alley covered with ivy and dead trees," and playhouses made out of the most random of materials (old boards, tree branches, cardboard boxes). When participants did identify an indoor location, most often it was their own room. Other special places within the home were closets, the space under their bed, and "underneath a blanket draped over the dining room table." Interestingly, 11 percent of the people who named a special place described a small compartment or closet located underneath a stairway.

In some ways, the tendency to select a personal space outside the house is a bit surprising. All of these participants were less than twelve years old when they found or created their special spot. At that age, their ability to roam far from home was likely limited. Moreover, it's not the case that children spend a great deal of time outside. On the contrary, studies find that children spend the vast majority of their day indoors.

This preference for an outdoor location most likely reflects the children's need to establish a special place independent of their parents. In the absence of parental supervision, children are free to arrange their place any way they want, to make their own rules, and to spend time as they please. There's no mother to tell them to straighten their room or to put away their toys. In fact, creating a place of one's own without parental intervention is the whole idea. A tree house or backyard fort erected and maintained by one's parents might make a nice play area, but it isn't the same as building a place on your own.

Participants' responses to follow-up survey questions confirmed that these special places served more functions than simply providing a place to play. I asked participants how they felt when visiting their special place and why they thought this place was special. The most common responses reflected a desire to exercise personal control, to do what they wanted without worrying about rules or the reactions of others. Here are their words:

> I had the power, since it was my playhouse.
>
> I felt free, older, and responsible for my own self.
>
> Even if people knew everything about me, they wouldn't be able to know me in my room. I guess it was the only thing I felt belonged to me.
>
> I could do and be anything I wanted because no one could see me or bother me.
>
> The fact that I could go there and do whatever I wanted and have no one bother me made it special. I felt in control of my own little-girl world.
>
> I could get away and do my own thing. Be who I wanted to be. I could be in my own world.
>
> I could make my own rules.
>
> We were kings of our own world.

Another theme that showed up repeatedly was the sense of security children experienced in their special place. Of the people in my study, 36 percent used the word "safe" or "secure" when describing how they felt in their personal place. In some cases, it was a place of refuge. As one man explained,

"I went there when I needed to feel safe and comforted. It released me from the family chaos outside my room."

Privacy was another common feature of these childhood places. Exactly half the participants who identified a special place said they usually or always were alone when they went there. Even when the space was shared by others, these were always close friends or relatives. For some participants, the place was special specifically because others did not or could not go there. "It was secretive," wrote one woman whose special place was a small enclosed area under the stairway. "It was a place where adults couldn't go because they weren't small enough."

Consistent Research Findings

The results from this one study confirmed my observation that children often find or create special places. I also found evidence that these places reflect the children's need to establish their own identity and a sense of mastery separate from their parents. Once again, I wondered if anyone else had studied this phenomenon. Given that I had found no previous research on people visiting childhood homes, I was not optimistic. However, this time an extensive search uncovered a small but relevant set of studies. Despite using different methods and studying different groups of people, in each case the findings were consistent with mine. I was also impressed that most of the research had been conducted outside the United States, suggesting that the tendency for children to find and create special places is not limited to this culture.

One of these studies was conducted by educator David Sobel. He made his observations when working in an elementary school in England and with children on the island of Carricau in the West Indies.[11] Sobel asked children age five and above to draw maps of their neighborhoods. The only requirement was that the children include their home on the map. The children also were instructed to include "the places that are special or important to you." The map-drawing exercise was followed by an interview in which the children identified the places on their maps and explained what made them special.

Sobel found that the majority of the children in both countries identified their own private places, what he called "forts, dens and bush houses." These special places could be any location the child found or built that provided some seclusion: a clearing in a wooded area, a structure built out of scrap wood and debris, or a bed of tramped-down weeds in the middle of a field. Sobel also asked some of the English children to take him to their special places. He discovered that the children's secluded hideaways actually "were often very close to home and in very public locations. But it became clear to me that in the children's eyes, these places were outposts in the wilderness."[12] Like the Americans in my study, the English and West Indian children felt as if they owned their special place and that it was their refuge for thinking and letting their imaginations run wild.

Clare Cooper Marcus, a professor of architecture, investigated children's special places during her work with adults.[13] She led some of her students on a "guided fantasy tour back to a favorite childhood place." As in previous studies, most of the students readily identified a private, secluded location that had captured their imagination and had served as a place of refuge and discovery. Cooper Marcus asked her students to close their eyes and explore this place in their imaginations. Then she asked them to sketch and describe it. When Cooper Marcus analyzed the students' descriptions, two common features emerged. First, like the participants in my study, most identified a favorite childhood place that was largely or partly outdoors. Only 14 percent described an indoor location. Second, also like my participants, the students recalled that their special place was private—or at least what the children considered private at the time. Although occasionally shared with one or two other children, more often the special location was limited to its creator or discoverer. In no case were parents allowed inside.

Finally, Finnish researcher Kalevi Korpela asked nine- and twelve-year-olds in Tampere, Finland, to identify their "favorite place" and to answer several questions about it.[14] Although the researcher did not ask specifically about a special place the children thought of as their own, many of the children nonetheless identified a place that allowed them a significant degree of privacy. Other children selected places that allowed them to clear their minds, relax, say what they wanted, and share secrets with friends. In short, when asked about their favorite place in their world, many of these Finnish children selected a location that sounds very much like the special places children described in other studies.

What makes a place special to children this age? David Sobel, the researcher who interviewed children in England and the West Indies, identified six features common to such places.[15] Although not every special place possesses all six of these characteristics, when considered together, it's easy to see why a child would develop an attachment to such a place.

1. Special places are found or constructed by children on their own.
2. Special places are secret.
3. Special places are owned by their creators.
4. Special places are safe.

5. Special places are organized worlds.
6. Special places empower their builders.

Another key characteristic of these special places is that their existence always seems to be limited to the same age range. In each study I found, participants either were between the ages of five and twelve or described experiences from this time in their lives. But this observation raises another question: is it possible that children younger than five also find and develop special places but are prevented by childhood amnesia from recalling the experience? Within their confined worlds, do these young children also seek out secluded corners or construct rudimentary forts?

To answer this question, one team of investigators asked three- to five-year-old children attending day care if they had "a special place in the center that belongs just to you?"[16] If children said yes, the researcher asked them to show him or her the place and to describe what they did there. Anyone who has worked with children this age understands that this type of investigation is fraught with difficulties, most particularly whether the child's understanding of "special place" and "belongs just to you" matches what the investigator has in mind. Nonetheless, fifty-five out of one hundred children were able to show the researcher a place they identified as special to them. However, only a few of these places resembled the kind of private, hideaway spots common among older children. Most often, the children identified places where they liked to play or a table where they liked to work. Of course, the opportunities for preschool children to hide (or think they are hiding) from adults are, and should be, quite limited. But the findings suggest that the need to locate and maintain a private, kids-only place probably doesn't surface until a little later in life.

Why Visit This Home?

Back to the question I posed at the beginning of the chapter. Specifically, of all the places people become attached to during their life, why is their home from the elementary school years the one they most often want to visit? Because of childhood amnesia, it is easy to understand why a home lived in prior to age five would not be very interesting. But beyond this, I think there are three reasons behind the preference for homes lived in between the ages of five and twelve.

First, the unique way children interact with their physical environment during these preteen years most likely leads to especially strong emotional bonds with these worlds. Much like with a first love, people recall with great fondness the old neighborhood, backyard, and fishing hole. As I explained in the previous chapter, the human tendency to view the past through rose-tinted glasses probably makes these childhood memories more pleasant than they actually were. Nonetheless, many people feel a powerful urge to visit the places where these memories were formed, if for no other reason than to experience the emotions once again.

Second, the way elementary school children interact with their worlds goes hand in hand with their development of a sense of individuality and personal identity. Moreover, as described in the previous chapter, people often tie their sense of self to significant places, particularly to their home. In a way, bits and pieces of your self are scattered about your childhood home and the surrounding area. What better way to get in touch with the person you once were than to return to the old neighborhood and dredge up those memories and emotions?

Third, there is a widespread belief in our culture that childhood years are filled with life-shaping experiences. Most Americans attribute their personalities, values, emotional temperaments, and other personal characteristics at least in part to what they went through during their "formative years." Family dynamics, especially parents' actions, are frequently invoked to explain ambitiousness, shyness, emotional dependence, and so forth. Indeed, among the people I interviewed, 25 percent spontaneously introduced the notion of their formative years, and 34 percent described how certain childhood experiences had an impact on them. Given this widespread belief, it's not surprising that people who want to reconnect with their past would turn to the place where they believe these significant events happened.

CHAPTER FOUR

A Place to Be

In 1982, when Johnny Carson was the undisputed king of nighttime television, NBC aired a prime-time special titled *Johnny Goes Home*. The program featured nothing more than Johnny's return to Norfolk, the small town in northeastern Nebraska where he grew up. Driving his father's restored 1939 Chrysler, Johnny pointed out his father's office, the YMCA where he spent afternoons swimming and playing basketball, and the furniture store where he held a part-time job. While walking down the streets of Norfolk, he visited the store where he bought his first bicycle, the barbershop where he used to get his hair cut, and the five-and-dime where the manager once caught him trying to steal a cheap ring. Viewers also were shown Johnny's high school and his "secret hideaway" by the river where he used to swim and fish and just spend time alone.

Of course, the show also featured the house, where the son of the current owners led Johnny and the television audience on a tour. To Johnny's delight, the place had changed very little. He pointed out the fireplace his father had built and the corner where the large radio used to stand. He laid on the floor to demonstrate how he used to listen to Jack Benny and other favorites. Seeing the room that he shared with his brother brought to mind the pigeons that used to flutter outside the bedroom window. Shooting baskets in the driveway reminded him of how he used to shovel snow from that same driveway during the cold Nebraska winters.

What I find most intriguing about this broadcast is that the people in charge of programming at NBC believed Johnny Carson's visiting his childhood home would make good television. And, in fact, millions of viewers did tune in.[1] Of course, Johnny Carson was a celebrity, the man who brought laughter and entertainment into millions of American homes each night. But Johnny told no jokes during the special. He was on a personal journey, not entertaining. So, where is the appeal? Johnny explained it this way:

> I think everyone gets a little homesick. Especially if you have fond memories of your early years, and I do. You want to visit old, familiar places, visit with some of your former classmates. And return for a least a moment to an era that gave you a direction in your life. You know, in a world that changes rapidly, I guess what one looks for in returning home is a link with something permanent, a sense of belonging.[2]

Johnny Carson's reflections and experiences resemble in many ways those of others who visit childhood homes. The people we interviewed described an emotional pull, the return of memories, and the joy of discovering something familiar. They talked about distinctive sounds and smells, the soil and the trees, and the satisfaction of getting back in touch with the past. Many of their stories appear in the next three chapters. But let's begin with the question of why people take these trips.

Three Reasons to Visit

As described in chapter 1, no matter what part of the country I sampled, I found that roughly one-third of all Americans over the age of thirty have visited a childhood home with the specific intent of seeing the physical places from their youth. To better understand this phenomenon, I used a fairly simple approach. Essentially, I asked people to describe their experiences. In total, my research assistants and I interviewed more than a hundred individuals who had made such a trip. We taped the interviews and then independently listened to the tapes, recording and counting statements we thought psychologically meaningful. We also kept our ears open, listening for insights and observations that otherwise might not have occurred to us.

For the most part, we allowed participants to tell their own stories. But we also came armed with a list of questions we wanted to explore. If, toward the end of the interview, participants had not addressed these topics on their own, we asked. Chief among our questions was simply why they had made the trip.

While reviewing the interviews, my assistants and I soon identified three main reasons participants gave for visiting their childhood homes. Although some people talked about more than one reason, we had little difficulty placing most of our participants into one of three categories. The largest of these we called "connection." People in this category described the trip as an opportunity to establish a psychological or emotional connection with their past. They made up 42 percent of the participants we interviewed. The second category we called "current issues." Participants placed in this group visited their childhood home specifically to help with problems and issues they faced in their current lives. These people comprised 15 percent of our sample. Finally, 12 percent of the individuals we spoke with fell into the "unfinished business" category. Participants in this group returned to their former home as part of a process of working through issues that remained from childhood.

We made the decision to be more exclusive than inclusive when placing people into categories. That is, we wanted to include only "pure" cases rather than to place participants into categories because they almost belonged or because we didn't know where else to put them. As a result of this strategy, 31 percent of our participants were not classified into any of the three groups. Although these individuals expressed many of the same feelings and insights as the classified participants, we opted to examine relatively clear examples to better understand the three primary reasons that lead people to visit childhood homes.

This chapter focuses on people who visited a childhood home primarily to establish a sense of connection. These participants used a variety of phrases and expressions to explain the reasons for their visit. Without prodding from us, quite a few actually used the word "connect" or "connection" to describe the experience. Here are some examples:

> There's a sense of safety and security when things remain the same. Sometimes when you go back, you have a connection with a place, and that provides a sense of endurance.

> You know how kids carve their name on a desk or a tree to prove they were there? I guess it comes down to saying, "I was here." You want to feel that you were there, that you really existed. It was so long ago, you sometimes lose track of that.

> As you get older, naturally you think about what things were like fifty years ago. It wasn't a particularly delightful time in my life, but it was a time full of

> memories. You want to recall those memories. You want to feel like it's all a part of your life, even the time when you were just a child.
>
> The trip was really just a connection with the past and a jumping off point for the future. In the hustle and bustle of everyday life, you kind of lose track of where you're coming from and where you're supposed to be going. The trip helped me get in touch with that.
>
> It's a place where I can access my childhood better than anywhere else. I tuck it away in my heart until I return.

The Starting Point: Feeling Disconnected from the Past

In one way or another, everyone we placed in the connection category decided to visit a childhood home after perceiving a lack of connection with the past. In a few cases, participants were unable to put their finger on exactly what motivated them until after the trip. They talked about feeling nostalgic or a vague yearning to see the old home and neighborhood. But most of our participants had a fair understanding beforehand that they had somehow lost touch with an important part of who they are and thought that visiting their childhood home would provide at least a partial remedy for this unsettling feeling.

Most commonly, a single event triggered this awareness. One man opened his mail to find the *Class Update* book from his twenty-year high school reunion. He had not attended the event but was eager to see what had happened to his former classmates. However, as he read about the different paths people's lives had taken, he felt less and less connected to the people who had once formed his circle of friends. He had gone away to college, moved several times, and now found himself three thousand miles from his hometown. The man retrieved his high school yearbook from a dusty closet corner and turned to his own entry. As he read about his activities and awards, he realized that he felt no more connected to this high school senior than to anyone else in the book. A few days later, he made plans for a trip.

This sense of disconnection had snuck up on many of our participants. For years they had given no thought to visiting their former homes, and then suddenly the desire was overpowering. Of course, the thread that connected these individuals with their childhoods had been thinning for a long time, but it wasn't until they stumbled across an old letter or photograph that they realized something was missing. The experience is consistent with what psychologists know about memory. Most of us believe our memories are far better than they really are. We assume a clear recollection of past events and places, only to discover that our memories are spotty at best when we are forced to recall specific information.

One participant came to this realization when she was working on an assignment in a genealogy class. The instructor asked her to draw the floor plan of the house she had lived in as a child. Although it had been thirty-two years since she had last seen that home, she was dismayed to discover that she had forgotten where some of the furniture had been or even where some of the rooms were located. After hearing this story, I asked five of my friends to try the same exercise. None had seen his or her childhood home in more than twenty years. Although they all thought the task would be simple, four of the five discovered significant gaps in their memories. One woman could not recall where the door to the backyard was located. Another could not remember the number of bedrooms in the house. Like the woman in the genealogy class, my friends found these holes in their memories upsetting.

In a few cases, participants discovered this lack of connection when they happened upon their old neighborhoods. One man was passing through his hometown on a business trip to New Jersey. He took a detour a few miles off his planned route to drive by the house he had not seen in twenty-three years. His first surprise was the difficulty he had finding the place. He had spent his entire childhood exploring this neighborhood, but it took him a couple of wrong turns before he found his way to the former home. The next surprise was how much he had forgotten—the red bricks on the front of the house, the elm tree that shaded the entire front lawn, and the fact that his bedroom window had faced the street. Two months later, he made a trip specifically to take a longer look.

Another participant grew up in Guam and moved to the U.S. mainland when he was twenty. Nine years later, he returned to the island for his father's funeral. Typical of people in their twenties, he had given little thought to his childhood home. But when his plane approached the island, he was overcome with emotion: "I was looking out the window and I started seeing the lights. And little tears started coming down. And I said, 'Wow. Home.' I cried to myself. It was good to be back. It was a feeling of relief, like there was a weight lifted off my shoulders. Just to be there made me feel good."

Pulitzer Prize–winning author and playwright William Saroyan described a similar experience. Saroyan spent much of his life traveling and lived in a variety of large cities, including San Francisco, New York, and Paris. In his late sixties, Saroyan wrote *Places Where I've Done Time*, a memoir describing sixty-eight places that held special memories for him.[3] One of these vignettes relates his decision to move back to Fresno, California, where he had spent most of his elementary school years:

> In 1963 I had done a lot of living and traveling, and I thought it would be pleasant to go back to my hometown, my birthplace, Fresno, and feel some of the summertime ease I had felt when I had been there long ago, from 1915 to 1926, in fact—ten years of very great importance in my life. I drove down from San Francisco in a little red Karmann-Ghia I had bought in 1959 in Belgrade, and I parked the car just a little outside the heart of town. I walked around and looked at places I hadn't looked at in many years. I didn't go to a hotel or motel, because I wasn't sure I wanted to hang around longer than an hour or two. . . . It was very hot. I found a place with root beer on tap. There were bees flying around and lighting on the spigot of the big barrel from which the root beer was drawn. And that did it. The flavor of the cool, foamy root beer did it, or at any rate made me decide that this heat was mine and I had better have some of it again.

The next day, Saroyan bought a house in Fresno (two houses, in fact, because "the house next door seemed to have a good floor plan") and two weeks later moved back to his hometown.

Success Stories: Reconnecting with the Past

After allowing participants to describe their experiences, one of the first questions we asked was, Do you consider the trip a success? Although many described mixed feelings, the vast majority of our participants found the trip rewarding and satisfying. Of the people in the connection group, 83 percent said they were definitely glad they had taken the trip. This figure is particularly impressive when we realize that, despite an average of eighteen years since they last saw their childhood home, most people stayed only a day or two.

What people did after they arrived also provides clues about their reasons for the trips. Of course, the focal point of everyone's visit was the actual building in which he or she had lived as a child. But almost no one stopped there: 79 percent in the connection category spontaneously mentioned that they had also looked around the old neighborhood. This entailed more than simply driving through the area to reach their former home. Rather, these individuals made an effort to locate specific sites or at least to walk around recalling who had lived there and what had happened here. Many sought out their best friend's house, a place that evoked memories of after-school adventures, sleepovers, and important conversations. Others looked for favorite play areas—fields, parks, empty lots. Of course, not everyone grew up in an urban or suburban environment. One participant walked through the orchards that surrounded her parents' farmhouse. Another sought out the abandoned mines in the hills behind his former home. Although it's a chilling thought for most parents today, the mines had been this man's favorite play area when he was a child.

Of the participants in the connection category, 62 percent visited at least one school they had attended. After home, school is probably the place where children spend the largest part of their days. Not only is school the scene for many important social encounters, but it also provides the setting for many early successes and failures, some of which carry emotional weight into adulthood. Although a few participants simply parked their cars outside the school yard and reminisced, most made an effort to walk onto the school grounds. Because many visited in the summer or on weekends, classes were not in session. Most of our participants attempted to locate former classrooms. Doors were rarely open, but most rooms had windows to peek through. Participants also sought out gymnasiums, cafeterias, and athletic fields. More than a few climbed on playground equipment. One man walked into the office of his former high school and asked to see old yearbooks, a request the administrative assistant readily granted.

Stores and businesses also played a role in many participants' childhoods. Of those in the connection category, 55 percent spontaneously mentioned visiting some type of store or place of business. Grocery stores were common destinations. Ice cream parlors, drive-ins, donut shops, and other places to hang out also were mentioned frequently. Quite a few people ordered a milk shake, ice cream cone, or some other favorite treat from their youth.

Of the connection participants, 14 percent reported visiting a cemetery, a place well-suited for the kind of reflection many of them sought. Other locations mentioned by more than one participant included churches, libraries, and movie theaters. Several participants made a point to visit a place where they had once held a job, although more often than not the store or business no longer existed.

In addition to these common destination points, many participants sought out places that had special meaning just for them. Some returned to the site of a childhood achievement. Sometimes these were scenes of public recognition, such as the stage where a spelling bee was held or the football field where a championship was won. But more often, our participants were interested in personal accomplishments. One man returned to the pool where he had learned to swim. He had been afraid of the water until long after the other boys and girls his age were swimming in the deep end of the pool.

He eventually became a member of his high school swim team. Another participant had suffered from extreme shyness throughout childhood. Then, during his first year of high school, a teacher convinced him to get involved in drama. The experience changed the way he looked at himself more than his teacher could have imagined. The man went on to study acting in New York before eventually turning to a career as a pharmacist. Decades later, he returned to his old high school and walked on the familiar stage. Looking out into the empty auditorium, he was overcome with emotion. That participant was sixty-nine when we spoke with him. In his retirement, he had returned to acting in community productions.

The most vivid memories from one participant's childhood were the summer afternoons and evenings he and his friends spent playing baseball in their neighborhood park in New Jersey. Whenever a business trip takes him nearby, he schedules enough time to visit the old neighborhood and, in particular, the old ballpark. "I walk on the field where I used to play shortstop," he explained. "I go between second and third and kind of kick the dirt and maybe get down in a crouch and make like I'm fielding a grounder."

Several participants in the connection category talked about insights and perspectives they gained from the experience and lessons they brought home with them. Lydia had no illusions that the central California house she had grown up in was anything but substandard. From the time she was six until she moved away at twenty-one, her family lived on her grandparents' farm in a structure originally used as a chicken coop. There was no heating or indoor plumbing. It didn't take long before Lydia saw other children's homes and became ashamed of where she lived. She was too embarrassed ever to invite over friends from school.

Thirty years later, Lydia was living in a comfortable house with her husband and son when it suddenly dawned on her that she wanted to see the old house again. The desire to visit was powerful but perplexing. "I decided that I wanted to go back," she said. "But I didn't know what I was trying to do. I know I was trying to fill a need with seeing the place. But I wasn't sure what need that was."

So, Lydia and her family made the drive back to the farm that had once belonged to her grandparents. Predictably, the old chicken-coop-turned-home was gone. The new owners seemed to remember that it had burned down a few years earlier. But they allowed Lydia to look around the property, and she led her family on a search for traces of her past. The first thing she found was a grove of familiar trees, then part of a ditch that used to run by the old house. Relying on a few remaining landmarks and her memory, Lydia drew an outline in the soil where the house had once stood. She gathered her family inside the empty space and shared with them the onslaught of childhood memories that followed.

Not finding the house intact had been disappointing but not unexpected. Nonetheless, while standing on the ground where her childhood home had once been, Lydia understood why she had made the trip. She needed to get back in touch with what it was like to grow up in such poverty. Starting that day, she no longer thought of her background as shameful but rather as a point of pride. She had wanted to take her family along, she realized, to show them how far she had come and what she had accomplished in her life.

An Unexpected Observation: Trees

Like many writers, historian and essayist Loren Eiseley experienced the urge to visit his childhood home. Eiseley waited sixty years to return to the small Nebraska town where he had grown up. But it was not the house or the neighborhood that called him back. Rather, it was a tree. Eiseley and his father had planted a cottonwood sapling in the front yard more than six decades earlier. "We'll plant the tree here, son," his father had said. "And when you're an old, old man you can sit under it and think how we planted it here, you and me, together."[4]

As it turns out, Eiseley's attachment to the cottonwood is far from uncommon. Soon after we began talking with people about their visits, my research assistants and I recognized a common theme in the stories we heard. Without any prompting from us, person after person mentioned trees. Many described the trees that grew in their neighborhood park or that filled the mountains near their former homes. But more often, they identified a specific tree or grove of trees that they had treasured as a child. When we analyzed the tapes from our interviews, we found that 56 percent of our participants had spontaneously mentioned trees when talking about their visits.

Why might this be the case? After listening to the way our participants described the trees from their childhood, we came up with several answers to this question. First, trees are relatively permanent. A history professor once pointed out to me that the maple trees outside my office are more than two hundred years old. The American Indians who once inhabited the area walked in the shade of these trees, as did the people who founded the university where I work and nearly every student and professor who has passed through the school throughout its history. Barring ecological disaster, the trees will be here for students to walk beneath long after I retire. It's this kind of permanence people often seek when they visit a childhood home. They want some kind of reassurance that the place where they once lived and played retains a physical presence, even though their childhoods are now relegated to memory. People accept that friends grow up and move away and that parents get older and pass on. But they find satisfaction in knowing that the tree they once climbed is still standing and will continue to stand, dropping the same fruit in the summer and the same leaves in the fall.

Second, something about trees makes them particularly apt for use as symbols. Writers and poets have seen trees as metaphors for life, family, strength, nature, and endless other concepts. It is reasonable to suggest that children also come to think of trees symbolically, even if they are not always aware of the associations. One woman recognized that the apple tree outside her bedroom window had become her symbol for safety and security. As a child, the tree had often provided a peaceful view to offset her stressful family life. It had even served as an avenue of escape from her second-story room, when using the front door meant interacting with her parents. "As long as that tree was there," she said, "I knew that I would be alright. I knew that no matter how bad things got at home, there was another side to things. A peaceful and safe side that would always be there for me."

Third, because of their physical prominence, beauty, and accessibility, trees are often associated with fond childhood memories. As described in chapter 3, tree houses frequently become special, private places where children develop a sense of individuality and independence. Sometimes, as with essayist Loren Eiseley, the tree was planted ceremoniously in the presence of loved ones. One participant became especially emotional when he saw the large fir tree standing in front of his childhood home. It had been more than fifty years since he had last seen the place. "My sister had planted that tree when we were just children," he said. "And there it was, a big, tall fir tree now. All I could think about was my sister, how she had grown up in that house and lived in that town all her life." The sister had died a few years earlier, but the man found satisfaction in knowing that her tree continued to tower like a monument in front of the old wooden house where they had shared a childhood.

Grabbing a Piece of the Past: Souvenirs and Mementos

Most of our participants required more than one visit to their childhood home to fully satisfy their need to connect with the past. Many had already made a second (or third or fourth) trip by the time we spoke with them. In fact, 73 percent of the participants in the connection category said they either had made another trip to the same childhood home or that they hoped to go back some day.

But repeated trips or the promise of returning some day was not sufficient to satisfy the need for connection for many people. Some of the individuals we spoke with needed a tangible, physical reminder of their childhood home. Of our participants, 22 percent took cameras with them during their initial trip. Several brought their photographs to the interview, much the way proud parents eagerly show off pictures of their children. Others said they regretted not bringing a camera along (most of these trips were made before cell phones routinely came with cameras). They vowed to carry one the next time they visited.

A number of people returned literally with pieces of their childhood homes. One man took a chip of concrete out of the driveway where he and his brothers used to play basketball. Another man brought back the rusted flag from the mailbox that once stood in front of the house. Other participants returned with paint chips, pieces of brick, tree bark, and stones. Several brought back small samples of soil. One woman kept a small glass jar filled with soil from her former backyard on her desk. "Sometimes I feel better just pouring it into the palm of my hand," she said. "I feel like I'm physically in touch with the place." Much like the souvenirs people keep from vacations, weddings, and sports events, these physical reminders seemed to provide our participants with a symbolic yet tangible link to something important.

Visiting a Childhood Home As a Source of Creative Inspiration

Fiction writers frequently set their stories in locations where they have lived, often in their hometowns. One obvious reason for this choice is that they are following the oft-cited advice to "write what you know." But conversations with writers suggest that they often select these locations for other reasons. Authors of literary fiction in particular are interested in exploring their observations about the human condition. If we think of a childhood home as an extension of the self, then a fiction writer's hometown is perhaps an ideal location for getting in touch with events that gave rise to the writer's perceptions of the world.

Early in his career, I asked Pulitzer Prize–winning author Michael Chabon why he selected Pittsburgh as the setting for his first two novels. He explained that the choice was not simply a matter of convenience:

> I think I return to Pittsburgh because it was the city where I grew up, physically, emotionally, sexually, etc. It was the setting for *Mysteries* [*of Pittsburgh*, my first novel] because that was a novel about growing up. It was probably the

> setting of *Wonder Boys* because . . . I needed to retreat to a familiar place. . . . I had spent 4 1/2 years writing a book that took place in Paris and Florida. That book just never came together, and I was so bruised by the experience that I think I needed the familiarity of Pittsburgh.[5]

William Styron, another Pulitzer Prize winner, also found renewed inspiration by placing his fictional characters in a familiar setting. After a fifteen-year hiatus from publishing fiction, Styron wrote *A Tidewater Morning*. As the title suggests, the setting for the work is the Tidewater area of Virginia, where Styron grew up. He explained the choice:

> I have always felt that I've been drawn back to my origins as a writer, even when I have been dealing with far-flung subjects or subjects that are not relative to that region of the country. I think writers are often very much a product of their roots and tend to gravitate backwards toward those roots, and therefore I have always felt that in most of my work there was a reflection of my first 20 years or so.[6]

In chapter 3, I mentioned Edith Cobb's notion that creative thinkers often seek out the spontaneous, open-eyed view of the world they experienced regularly as children. Although Cobb never advocated physically returning to a childhood home, my research suggests that creative people might benefit from the experience. Anecdotal evidence from individuals known for their creativity also supports this conclusion.

Every few years, Woody Allen makes a trip to the Brooklyn neighborhood where he grew up. His chauffeur parks on a side street a few blocks away and waits while the famous actor and director makes the trip on foot.[7] These trips help Allen retain the strong connection he feels with his childhood. As he told a biographer, "As I've grown older, my life has developed a more tangible continuity with my childhood than most people's. In my mind, it was only yesterday that I was standing in line to enter the school building. It's not that I just remember it like it was yesterday, I have a feeling for it. It's not ancient history in any way. I feel I'm still spinning out from that experience."[8]

In two of Woody Allen's movies, the main character also visits the home where he grew up. In *Annie Hall*, the trip provides a bit of nostalgia and a vehicle for humor. In *Crimes and Misdemeanors*, the visit is an important step in the character's attempt to deal with a current life crisis. We'll discuss people who visit former homes for this reason in the next chapter.

The late playwright August Wilson (yet another Pulitzer Prize recipient) credits his play *Jitney* to the inspiration he received when visiting his old Pittsburgh neighborhood.[9] Perhaps not coincidentally, most of Wilson's plays are set in and around the streets where he grew up. To Ernest Gaines, author of *The Autobiography of Miss Jane Pittman* and *A Lesson before Dying*, visiting his childhood home was more than inspirational; it was a necessity. Gaines spent the first fifteen years of his life in rural Louisiana. As a black man, he was pleased to move to Northern California in the late 1940s to escape the racism of the South. The former slave quarters he and his family lived in have long been torn down, but he keeps a picture of the cabin hanging in his San Francisco apartment. Today Gaines is a respected novelist and a winner of the National Book Critics Circle Award. But there was a time in the early 1960s when he was just another struggling writer. That's when it dawned on him what he needed to do: "I was trying to be a writer, struggling to be a writer, without ever going back to the South, to the source of what I was trying to do. I did not want to do it. And then I went back and I spent six months there, and I think that saved . . . my writing career."[10]

Gaines's novels were written in his apartment in San Francisco, but each is set on a fictional Louisiana sugarcane plantation similar to the one on which he was born. Throughout his career, Gaines has frequently visited his childhood home, often twice a year. He takes a camera with him and sometimes looks at the photographs when he writes. "A writer can write about a certain time and that's it," Gaines once told a reporter. "My soul, my spiritual home, is Louisiana. . . . I always go back to it, and at the same time I wish I never do."[11]

Sharing the Experience with Others

Among the important decisions we make when interacting with others is how much and what to reveal about ourselves—what psychologists call self-disclosure. Numerous studies find that we typically reveal personal information in a selective manner.[12] That is, we talk freely about superficial topics with people we have just met, but we limit conversations about more intimate topics—fears, dreams, insecurities—to those we are close to. When researchers examine conversations between strangers, they find a tendency to start with "safe" topics like movies, sports, and that old standby, the weather. But as the conversation continues, people gradually move toward more personal subjects, perhaps talking about things that worry them or parts of themselves they would like to improve.

Relationships develop in a similar manner. First-date conversations include descriptions of work, favorite actors, and vacations. But as two people get to know and like one another, it is expected that each will become comfortable disclosing personal experiences and feelings. In fact, failure to share personal information can sabotage a healthy relationship. Not only do we disclose personal information to those we like, but sharing intimate information often enhances the bond between people.[13] Thus, one way to take a relationship to a deeper level is to share intimate thoughts and emotions. Researchers also find that women tend to self-disclose more often than men.[14] This gender difference is consistent with other studies that find American women are more focused on personal relationships and social intimacy than are men.

If we think of a childhood home as an extension of the self, then sharing a visit to that home also can be seen as an act of self-disclosure. Showing someone close to you where you used to live—and sharing the stories and memories the visit evokes—is a powerful way to reveal an important part of yourself.

Nonetheless, I was surprised by the large number of participants who took someone with them when visiting their childhood home. Because the experience is similar to the kind of self-exploration that people usually engage in on their own,[15] I had anticipated that the vast majority would make the trip alone. However, only about half the people we interviewed made their initial visit to a childhood home by themselves; 48 percent took someone with them on their journey. When we look at each of the three categories separately, an even more interesting pattern emerges. People who made the trip primarily to deal with current life issues went by themselves 67 percent of the time. Similarly, 63 percent of those who returned to complete unfinished business from childhood went alone. Because people in both of these groups were wrestling with personal issues, these were the kinds of numbers I had expected.

In contrast, 62 percent of those who visited a childhood home with the primary intent of connecting with their past took someone with them. In most cases, the companions were spouses or children, but a few brought along siblings, boyfriends or girlfriends, parents or grandchildren. In addition, several participants who went alone the first time they made the trip brought someone with them on a subsequent visit. Consistent with the research on self-disclosure, women were more likely to share the experience than were men. Whereas 69 percent of the women in the connection category took a companion with them, only 56 percent of the men did so.

Most of the participants who made the trip with a spouse or romantic partner talked about sharing something important with that person. One woman took her new husband to see the Idaho town where she had grown up. "I knew everything about him, but he didn't really know my background—where I played and things like that," she said. "Now when I talk about things in my past, he knows about them. I felt so much closer to him after that trip."

In some ways, taking a loved one along is like letting that person read pages from a childhood diary. Conversations about relationships with parents and siblings flow easily when we are standing in front of a former home. Seeing a former schoolyard or walking by an old swing set can trigger discussions about childhood fears and accomplishments. In a few cases, the trip served as a kind of test for a new boyfriend or girlfriend. As one woman explained, "I wanted to see if he would still love me after seeing where I came from."

A few years ago, a graduate student waited around until the crowd cleared following a talk I had given on this topic. He wanted to tell me about a trip to the East Coast he had recently taken with his girlfriend with the specific purpose of showing her his hometown. He took her to the house he had lived in, the schools he had attended, and a few special places from his childhood. That evening they sat on a large boulder overlooking the ocean where he had spent countless hours during his youth. "She had to see my past and not just hear about it," he said. "Then she would really know who I was." As the sun set, he asked her to marry him.

A large number of participants took their children to see their former home, and many said they planned to take their children with them the next time they went. Most of these people talked about establishing a sense of connection across generations. One woman was concerned that her children had moved too often and had no place they could call home. So, she took them to see the house that had belonged to her parents and to her grandparents before that. "Since they've gone around to a lot of different homes, perhaps they could think of this as a home through the centuries," she said. "I would like them to have a sense of connectedness to their family and its history. I told them, 'This is a part of you too.'"

The Not-Always-Successful Trip: When Things Have Changed

Although most of the people we interviewed were delighted to discover that parts of their childhood home and neighborhood were still intact, nearly all also recognized some changes. Many of these changes would probably seem inconsequential to an outside observer, such as a different color trim on the house or a different kind of flower in the garden. Other times the changes were more substantial, such as adding a room onto the house or chopping down a treasured tree. Regardless of the aesthetic or practical improvement, in almost no case did participants think the changes were for the better.

Many people were disappointed to find that their old home and neighborhood had deteriorated over the years. They talked about unpainted buildings, leaning fences, unkempt yards, and graffiti. In some cases, the disappointment may simply have illustrated the fallibility of memory. Children typically don't notice how well or poorly homes and gardens are kept. Unpleasant details like chipping paint and tall weeds rarely appear in our childhood memories. But it is also the case that many neighborhoods do deteriorate. Derek was particularly saddened over what had happened to his old school in the thirty-two years since he had last seen it:

> The grammar school was not as big as I thought it was. And it didn't look too good. The playground in the back, which I had pictured as big and immense and very nice, was sort of small and caged-in with a big, high chain-link fence. It must have been ten or twelve feet high. And half the play yard was concrete. And the other half was gravel, which I didn't understand. You can't go out there like we did at recess and play games on gravel. And out in front there used to be this big promenade and porch all around, and it was gone. And there used to be these huge, huge sycamore trees, and they were all gone. The front was such a mess. It used to be so pretty.

Phil last saw his hometown when he and his wife moved away in their early twenties. When he was fifty-five, he got a call from his son, who had just visited the area on a business trip. The son told his father that the community did not look anything like the place he had heard so much about. Phil's wife was out of town, and he had a few days free. So, he bought an airplane ticket and was soon on his way to New York. He walked around the old neighborhood and compared what he saw with what he remembered:

> It was the heart of town, where I had worked as a young boy at the A&P food market. That was closed. That was now a sleeper-type furniture store. In fact, the area as I knew it—where the shopping center was—was sort of run-down. Mike's, the barber shop, was closed. That's where I got my hair cut as a kid. And when my older son was due to have his first hair cut, I took him in there. It was all boarded up. And across the street was Bertleson's Ice Cream Parlor, where I had worked when I was in high school. This old German man owned it. It was just a spiffy, sparkling place. You'd walk in, and everything would gleam. He made his own ice cream and all his own candy. As soon as I looked across the street I said, "He doesn't own it anymore." Because it was sort of dirty. So, I went across the street, and I walked into the place. And I talked to whoever the owner was. He said Mr. Bertleson had died a few years earlier, which I suspected because he was pretty old. And I had an ice cream cone. The ice cream was still good. But I remember when I worked for him. Every night when we closed up at 10:30, we had to mop all the floor. And all the cases were stainless steel. You had to wash them down with real ammonia and

hot water. And all the mirrors. Every night. I don't think this place had been cleaned in a month of Sundays.

Virtually everyone who discovered large changes in their former home and neighborhood came away from the experience with mixed emotions. Although most of these participants found enough reminders to make the trip worthwhile, they could not suppress their feelings of disappointment and sadness. This reaction is not surprising for a couple of reasons. First, because the remnants of their former homes and neighborhoods were so different from their expectations, many participants found it difficult to connect with the past as they remembered it. The flood of memories most people experience was more like a trickle for those whose homes were barely recognizable. Many precious childhood memories remained buried.

Second, if people see places from their past as part of their self-concept, then the loss of a home or schoolyard as they remember it is also a personal loss. More than one participant compared their reaction to the way they felt when grieving for a loved one. "It was very sad," one woman said, "because you see a part of your life is gone. Now what you've called home is not home any more. So it's kind of like a man without a country. I have no place really to tie back to."

Finding that a childhood home has changed can be unsettling. Finding that the home no longer exists can be devastating. Unfortunately, this was the case for a few of our participants. Most were emotionally crushed by the discovery. As one man explained, "I would have been better off not knowing. As long as I believed the house was there, I felt like I could always go back to it if I wanted. It would have been so much better to think that way. Now when I think of my home and my childhood, I feel a big emotional void. It's like something's missing. I kind of think of it like a hole in my heart."

Consider the experience of Lawrence, whose fondest childhood memories were centered on the Oregon house he had lived in from ages six to nine. Before that time, he had moved around a lot and lived off and on with his grandparents. But his father returned one day, and for three years the two of them lived in what he remembers as a special place. "I wanted to see that house," he said. "I had so many happy memories. Those three years were very stable, and I had enormously good experiences. Like a broken arm. I fell off a bike, you know. All the good kid experiences. Batman comic books. And everything was fine."

Thirty years later, Lawrence felt a need to see the house again. The decision came a year after his divorce and, probably not coincidentally, a few months after his father's death. He thought about quitting his job in California and moving back to Oregon. He wanted to recapture something from his childhood. But when he made the trip, he could not have been more disappointed: "The home was gone. It was a vacant lot. The trees were chopped down. All the houses were gone. Only the street was still there. I fell into a very deep depression. That experience was such a depressing thing. Much more depressing than you could ever imagine. I couldn't stand it."

Lawrence left the scene immediately. Without the house, there was no reason to look through the community or the neighborhood. He checked into a nearby motel and stayed there the remainder of the week. It was to have been a week of discovery, of reconnecting with the happiest years of his life. Instead, it became a week of disillusionment and depression.

Fortunately, not all stories about missing homes have such unhappy endings. Jennifer's favorite place from childhood was the New England countryside where she and her family spent each summer. Her family owned two houses there, located next to a small lake and connected by a bridge. But when Jennifer made the trip thirty-three years after she had last seen the houses, they were gone. Only the bridge that once connected the two structures was still standing. The land had been sold to the state and converted into a park.

Jennifer was disappointed, but her determination to connect with her past was stronger than her discouragement. As she and her husband wandered around the property, she reconstructed the landscape from memory. She recognized many of the trees and pointed out the place where she had once buried a porcupine. The more she searched, the more she found:

> I went around looking for anything that would be personally meaningful to me that would still be there. I remembered that we'd had a rhubarb plant, and that every summer we'd go and we'd make different desserts with the rhubarb. I went looking for that. And that was still there. And there were other relics of my past. There was the mailbox that we had taken hikes to, to get the mail. And the irises that grandma planted, and the little orchard of apple trees that grandpa planted.

The biggest prize came when she found a pile of rubbish apparently discarded when the houses were torn down. She looked through the debris and found a white saddle shoe. Jennifer had no doubt the shoe was one she had worn as a child. Although not as satisfying as finding the houses she had hoped to visit, the shoe provided the link she was seeking—a physical trace of the happy summers from her childhood. "Something of endurance," she called it. Of course, she took the treasure home with her.

Loren Eiseley, the essayist who waited sixty years to seek out the tree he and his father had planted in their Nebraska home, also had to deal with disappointment. He found the house he grew up in still intact, but the cottonwood he and his father had planted was gone without a trace:

> I took a grasp on the picket fence and forced myself to look again. A boy with a hard bird eye of youth pedaled a tricycle slowly up beside me.
>
> "What'cha lookin' at?" he asked curiously.
>
> "A tree," I said.
>
> "What for?" he said.
>
> "It isn't there," I said, to myself mostly, and began to walk away at a pace just slow enough not to seem to be running.
>
> "What isn't there?" the boy asked. I didn't answer. It was obvious I was attached by a thread to a thing that had never been there, or certainly not for long. Something that had to be held in the air, or sustained in the mind, because it was part of my orientation in the universe and I could not survive without it. There was more than an animal's attachment to the place. There was something else, the attachment of the spirit to a grouping of events in time; it was part of our mortality.[16]

Unsuccessful Visits: Connection versus Return

The vast majority of people we placed in the connection category found their visits rewarding. This is not to say that they experienced only positive emotions or that the memories they encountered were all pleasant. But almost everyone considered the trip a success. When we asked at the end of the interview whether they might make another trip to see the same childhood home someday, nearly three out of four participants said they probably would.

However, we also found a few notable exceptions. Several people came away from the experience saddened and disillusioned. A few said bluntly that they wished they had never made the trip. These were not only individuals who discovered that their childhood homes were gone or changed substantially. Rather, a handful of participants had found their homes intact, yet still returned from their trips disappointed.

What about this small group made their reaction so different from the others? As I reviewed the transcripts, one answer jumped out at me. Each of these disillusioned participants had set out to do more than simply get in touch with the past. They wanted to return to the kind of life they had as children. In a sense, they sought to relive their childhoods. These participants did not want to connect with the past as much as they wanted to escape from the present. Each talked about how much better their lives had been when they were younger. Most considered the trip a first step toward moving back to their hometown. A few mentioned the possibility of moving back into the same house where they had spent their childhood.

Rudy remembered his childhood in a small Ohio town as the best time of his life. But his parents divorced when he was fifteen, and he and his mother moved to California. That's when everything changed. He spent five difficult years trying to adjust to his new situation. When he was twenty, he had a dream about his hometown. "Everything seemed so much more pleasant there. I was happier in Ohio than I was out here, so I thought maybe I could get in touch with those feelings if I went back."

He bought a car and made the trip. All along the way, he thought about how he was going to leave his troubles behind and return to the happiness he had known as a child. But within hours of arriving, he knew he had made a mistake. The people weren't as friendly as he remembered. The weather was more miserable than he had recalled, and he had forgotten all about the mosquitoes in the summer. The creek where he and his friends used to play was dammed up, and the trees that ran along the banks were gone.

Of course, the dammed-up creek and missing trees were only symbolic of the problem. Rudy could not play along the creek bed at age twenty like he had at age ten. And his old playmates were now adults with families, jobs, and adult interests. Rudy stayed in town just one night. He traveled around the Midwest for a while seeing some of the places he and his family had visited when he was a child. Eventually he ran out of money, sold his car, and hitchhiked back to California.

Rudy was fifty when we spoke with him and had not been back to Ohio since. Yet, he told us at the time that he still dreamed about his hometown almost every night. By the end of the interview, he seemed on the verge of recognizing what had gone wrong. "Maybe I have an unrealistic desire," he said. "Not to go back to my hometown so much as to go back to my youth. I was a carefree boy until I came out here. Sometimes I wonder if that's what I really want. To be a carefree boy again."

None of these disillusioned participants ever moved back to their hometown. This is probably fortunate, because trying to recreate a happy childhood is probably doomed from the start for several reasons. First, our memories are often inaccurate. Nostalgic ruminations about "the good old days" are usually pretty one-sided. We recall the happy experiences from childhood more readily than the unpleasant ones.[17] For most people, looking at the past through rose-colored glasses is probably good for their psychological well-being. However, as our disillusioned participants discovered, things often are not—and probably never have been—quite like the images in our memories. Second, it seems that these participants really wanted to escape from the responsibilities and challenges that come with adulthood. Although the thought of tossing adult concerns aside can be appealing at times, reality inevitably has the last word. Third, our disillusioned participants most likely were wrestling with adjustment and emotional issues that went beyond where to live. Had they moved, they probably would have packed up the underlying causes of their problems and brought them along to their new address.

Of course, it is possible for people to move back to the same town they knew as children and live a happy and productive life. I've encountered a number of individuals who talk about never losing their love of open spaces or who miss the excitement of a big city. But these people are not trying to run away from their problems. The difference between those who found visiting an intact childhood home satisfying and those who were disappointed probably comes down to this: those who found the trip rewarding incorporated their renewed sense of connection into their current lives. Rather than escaping from the present, these individuals used revived memories to strengthen the psychological thread that ties the present with the past.

Case Study: Ingrid

Ingrid grew up in a town of about five thousand people in a mountainous area that was then Germany but is now part of Poland. Her family lived in a grand house. The home was more than four hundred years old and had been recognized as a historic and architectural landmark. Ingrid spent most of her teenage years with World War II as a background. Still, the family stayed intact, and her memories of her hometown and the house where she grew up were for the most part quite pleasant. But the realignment of borders and restructuring of governments in Europe following the war changed everything. Her family was forced literally to flee with only the clothes on their backs. The government took the house and all their possessions. She was twenty years old and a refugee.

Eventually she settled in the United States. Political developments made a visit to her hometown difficult, if not impossible. But she never gave up hope of one day seeing the house again. "Always we were dreaming," she said. "All those years we were dreaming that one day we can go back. Someday we will go there." For forty-six years she dreamed.

Then, one day, she received a letter from her brother who also had immigrated to the United States. He had discovered a packaged tour of Germany and Poland that included a one-day stop in their hometown. Ingrid was so excited she could hardly stand it. "But I still had to wait seventy days," she said. "I got my ticket, and for seventy days I was always thinking, 'Oh, now finally! We can after forty-six years go and see our home!'"

The first day of the guided tour took them through Germany. She found East Germany run-down and depressing. But as the bus made its way toward Poland, she could see the mountains growing in the distance. "And then in the evening, we came to one mountain range," she recalled. "You got goose bumps. I felt so, I don't know. They took everything away from us, but the mountains they could not take away."

Finally the day came when the tour reached her hometown. Ingrid's emotions ran high as the bus approached her old neighborhood. "Before we came within one kilometer of the house, I felt my hair standing up," she said. "I was really feeling so funny." After almost half a century of waiting and dreaming, she was about to see her home.

But when the bus turned the familiar corner, the house was not there. "It was all so strange," she said. "Our house was gone. They built on our property about thirty little houses. We had a lake that was gone. The bus driver drove slowly, and I could see all of my hopes—everything I had thought—disappear. It was strange. I could not even cry. For forty-six years I had been waiting for that moment. It was such a letdown."

Ingrid and her brother waited a few days, then left the tour group and returned on their own to explore what remained of the old neighborhood. They discovered a mixture of the old and the new. The streets, like the town, now had Polish names. But some of the houses where their neighbors had lived were still standing. The more they searched, the more they found that looked familiar. Ingrid was particularly delighted to find a little railing by the creek that their father had built. They went into the nearby hills and found the caves where they used to play as children. They recognized names carved on the walls of the caves by some of the children they had grown up with. And then they discovered the spot where her brother had carved his name several decades earlier.

They spent two days looking for reminders of their past. They found the house where their grandparents had lived. It was run-down but still standing. They visited their former grade school, one of the few buildings that had been maintained over the years. Ingrid found the room where she had spent most of her grade school years, but it was Sunday, and the doors were locked. They visited the cemetery, but all the names were Polish. The German tombstones had been removed. Still, Ingrid snapped dozens of photographs. She brought a book of pictures with her to the interview.

Ingrid left Europe with mixed emotions. Finding a few little reminders of her childhood had been enthralling. But seeing how much was gone and how much had changed had been depressing. Moreover, she could not shake the feeling that something was wrong. It wasn't just that the house was missing or that so much had been changed and renamed. There was something else that didn't feel right, but at the time neither she nor her brother understood what it was.

A week after returning to her home in California, Ingrid was still sorting through her emotions. She started to jot down some thoughts about her trip, an exercise that grew into more extensive writing, and then into something that resembled a small book. One day as she was trying to put into words the way the town had looked, she suddenly realized what it was that had bothered her during the visit. She said,

> All of a sudden it dawned to me why was that strange feeling. Because there was not one bush, not one tree. It was all erased. And while I was writing this, I have been crying. I felt such a relief. I get it all out. And my husband came home and he said, "What's the matter?" And I couldn't stop crying. I knew then why. Before then I couldn't figure out why I was feeling so. Why I was so, so nothing. We looked to there for forty-six years, and now it was not like this. Maybe if our house would have been there.

We spoke with Ingrid eight months after her trip. In that time, she had come to accept the loss of her childhood home by focusing on the good parts of the visit. She made bound copies of her writing project and gave them as gifts to close friends and relatives. She brought one copy of her manuscript to the interview to share with us. And she was making plans for a return trip, this time with her two grandchildren, ages nine and twelve.

CHAPTER FIVE

A Place to Grow

Carrie Watts, the main character in the motion picture and play *The Trip to Bountiful*, has one goal before she dies. Geraldine Page received an Academy Award for her portrayal of the elderly woman who wants only to return to her childhood home in the rural town of Bountiful, Texas. Sharing crowded living quarters with her son and unpleasant daughter-in-law has made Mrs. Watts's life sad and unbearable. After years of trying, she finally eludes her family and, relying on the kindness of strangers, makes her way to Bountiful. But she finds only the remains of abandoned and decaying buildings where the town once stood. Nonetheless, she walks through what's left of her childhood home, noting the markings on the wall and reviving memories of her earlier life. At one point, she drops to her knees and feels the soil with her hands. When her son arrives to take her back, Mrs. Watts points out the unique color of the sky, the smell of the air, and the trees that will remain long after she and the buildings are gone. Her daughter-in-law asks if she plans to run away to Bountiful again. "I've had my trip," she answers. "And that's more than enough to keep me happy for the rest of my life."

Although fictional, Carrie Watts's experience is similar in many ways to the stories told by the people covered in this chapter. All of these participants found themselves at a point of crisis or at least a moment of decision. A few thought their lives were spinning out of control, but more often they simply felt directionless, sad, or unsure of themselves. Sometimes outside events brought them to a moment of transition. Others simply recognized that it was time for a change.

Of the people we interviewed, 15 percent fell into the current-issues category. Each of these individuals pointed to something they were wrestling with at the time of their visit that prompted the trip. Upon closer inspection, we found these participants could be placed into one of two subgroups. About half of our current-issues participants visited a childhood home largely to find meaning and direction in their lives. These people typically expressed a need to get in touch with "who I really am." Some described their lives as being offtrack. Others felt they had abandoned important principles and goals from an earlier time. The other half identified a specific event or crisis that triggered their desire to visit a childhood home. These events included a recent divorce, relationship problems, death of a loved one, loss of a job, and major health setbacks.

How can visiting a childhood home help people cope with or overcome this array of problems and issues? A few participants were able to articulate the connection fairly well:

> You have to figure out who you are. It's easy to get caught up in the day-to-day and lose sight of the basic values that make up the core of the person you are. If you don't stop to reflect on things like that every once in a while, you can find yourself acting in ways that are inconsistent with those values. You may not know why, but you'll know that what you're doing doesn't seem right. It's because you're not being true to yourself. That's why you have to go back every now and then to the beginning.

> Seeing the house gave me a profound sense of who I was. Of my real character. I don't know that I could have gotten in touch with that any other way. I had to put myself right back in the place. I had to reexperience what it was like to be me back then. Because of that, I had a much better idea of what I wanted in life—what I needed to do with my life to make me happy again.

Some participants described only a vague awareness that visiting the place where they grew up would somehow help them with their current struggles. Here's how two recalled their decision to make the trip:

> I'm not sure what I was hoping to find. I just figured that here was a place that held some remembrances from my past, and that sounded like something I should go find out about.

> I really can't say what made me go. But it had to do with my recent divorce, I was sure of that. That's the thing that started the whole trip.

Regardless of their reasons for making the trip, every participant we placed in the current-issues category said that he or she gained something valuable from the experience. In some cases, the insight came while visiting the former house and neighborhood. But more often, the information gleaned from the trip was but one step in a longer process of finding answers to some difficult questions. Based on what I now know about the experience of visiting a childhood home, it's easy to see why our participants found the trip so useful. If people want to get back to their roots—to rediscover the person they once were and the values they once held—there's no better way to revive memories from those early years than physically placing oneself in the spot where those memories were formed.

But which memories come forth depends in part on what the visitor is seeking. Participants who returned to the landscape of their childhood with questions about how they were raised, what they once held important, and what they learned from their upbringing were primed to retrieve memories relevant to answering those questions. Do you want to recall the moral lessons your parents taught you? Walking through the house where these lessons were delivered could very well trigger memories of the time your father lectured you about stealing a Hershey bar from the drug store or the guilt you felt when you broke your sister's skateboard and pretended you knew nothing about it.

Martin Landau portrayed this experience in the Woody Allen movie *Crimes and Misdemeanors*. Landau's character, renowned eye surgeon Judah Rosenthal, faces a serious moral dilemma. In a desperate moment, he has his mistress killed after she threatens to ruin his marriage and reputation by going public with their relationship. Shortly after the deed is done, he is overcome with remorse. Should he go to the police? More important, how can he reconcile his actions with his beliefs? As Judah wrestles with his conscience, he makes a trip to the house where he grew up. When the current owner allows him to walk around inside, Judah relives a Passover seder from his childhood. A young Judah quietly listens from his place at the table as the adults discuss questions of morality, integrity, and God.

Many current-issues participants talked about how the trip also provided time for contemplation and reflection. This was especially the case for those who made the visit alone—as the majority of the current-issues participants did—and when the trip required some long-distance driving. Miles of highway allow time to process the mountain of memories and emotions generated from seeing the old home and neighborhood. For most of our participants, these moments of reflection continued in the days and weeks that followed.

Finding a Direction in Life

Psychologists find that we often think of our lives as stories that begin in childhood and continue through the life cycle.[1] There are disappointments and surprises along the way, but when looked at as a whole, the entire experience comes together as some kind of coherent tale. When asked to tell their life stories, people describe more than an unconnected series of interesting events. They often point out how early experiences set them down certain paths that eventually shaped them into the kind of people they are today. Hardships are seen as tests and sometimes as blessings in disguise. In fact, reflecting on one's life can be therapeutic. Studies find that simply thinking about how much we've changed and improved over the years is an effective strategy for lifting our spirits.[2]

Most of our lives also contain natural checkpoints at which we stop to ask ourselves where we have been and where we are going. Psychologists often point to young adulthood, middle age, and the elderly years as times in the life cycle when individuals are most likely to address these questions. Not surprisingly, we found examples from each of these age groups among the current-issues participants.

Young Adults

During my many years of teaching college undergraduates, I've seen quite a few students wrestle with decisions about careers and other life-direction choices. Surveys find that today's college graduates select careers with an eye to making money more often than they did when I was a student. Nonetheless, the young men and women I work with often ask themselves how impending decisions about postgraduate education and employment line up with their values and principles. And those who make it through four years (or more) of college without addressing these questions often find the issues waiting for them upon graduation.

This is what happened to Roseanne. The usual college adventures kept her occupied and relatively content as she pursued her bachelor's degree. But the day she graduated, Roseanne experienced something of an emotional crisis. She had no job and no serious romantic relationship, no short-term goals and nothing to give her daily life structure. For the first time, Roseanne was truly free to decide what she wanted to do with herself and how she wanted to live. As some psychologists have observed, this kind of freedom can be unsettling.[3]

A vague instinct told Roseanne that the solution to her discontent might be found in her hometown. So, one evening she drove back to the Sacramento neighborhood where she had grown up. Although her family and friends still lived in the area, she decided not to contact any of them. Instead, she checked into a hotel and the next morning visited her old neighborhood. Her parents had sold the house, but she mustered the courage to knock on the front door. To her delight, the new residents allowed her to walk around inside.

The entire trip lasted less than twenty-four hours. As it turned out, the new owners had made dramatic changes to the inside of the house, to the point that Roseanne barely recognized it as the same building. At first she felt "violated," then "really sad." But her emotions changed as she reflected on the experience over the next few weeks. Eventually she came to see that she was spending too much time living in the past. On some level, she had harbored the notion that she might one day magically return to those happier times. She said,

> I wanted to be young and irresponsible again, and not have to deal with rent and car payments and work. But seeing all the changes in the house made me realize that I also needed to grow and change. But change into what? That also was something I got from seeing the house. It made me think a lot about what was important to me. When I was a kid living in that house, I had a lot of dreams. Somehow those dreams all disappeared, one at a time, until I found myself with a college degree and no ambition. But after just that one day, I started asking myself the right questions.

Middle-Aged Adults

Midlife seems like a logical time to take measure of how one's life is progressing. Of course, there is the proverbial midlife crisis in which the fortyish or fiftyish adult is ambushed by a sudden awareness of how old he or she has become. Affairs and red sports cars are said to follow. Less dramatically, after careers are established, a level of financial security attained, and families raised, people often ask how their lives have unfolded and what they still need to do to make their life stories satisfying ones. Erik Erikson, the famous psychoanalyst, described the decisions people face at this age in terms of generativity versus stagnation.[4] Although Erikson focused largely on the satisfaction that comes from influencing children and grandchildren, he and other psychologists observed the sadness that sometimes overtakes people at midlife. Without a sense of accomplishment or direction, daily existence can feel empty and boring.

Tamara visited her childhood home when she was forty-five, a trip that coincided with her youngest daughter's going off to college. She said,

> I don't know that I would call it an empty-nest kind of thing. It was more something that was building for a while. Being alone in that house sort of brought those ideas to the forefront. I thought, Well, you're not a kid anymore, but you're also not too old to do something important with your life. So I went through a period where I asked myself what I wanted to do with the remaining years I had. It wasn't really a bad time. In fact, it was kind of nice. It was like a break in my life when I finally had the time to think about what was important and what I really wanted.

Tamara's search eventually led her to the Southern California neighborhood she had lived in from age eight through high school. She explained,

> I still can't tell you what it was that got me to go back to that old house. But I know it had something to do with trying to get the big picture. You can't just forget about your childhood. I mean, good or bad, it has an influence on who you are. And so it's probably good to get in touch with all that. Pretending it didn't happen and acting like your life just started when you turned eighteen is just being ridiculous. I knew if I was going to get a grip on my life, I had to get a better idea of just what my life had been up to that point.

When asked if the visit had provided the answers she sought, Tamara replied, "Absolutely. Not everything, of course. But a whole lot of good insights. It helped me remember a lot of important things."

Elderly Adults

As people move into the later years, they often feel a need to weave their life experiences into a satisfying story. Unlike younger adults who focus on where their lives are headed, elderly individuals look for the coherent threads that hold their lives together. They seek out what Erikson called ego integrity—a sense of satisfaction about how their life story has unfolded. As for Carrie Watts in *The Trip to Bountiful*, that search sometimes includes a visit to a home they have not seen in several decades.

Arthur was seventy when he decided to visit the Midwestern farm where he had spent his childhood. He said,

> I wasn't expecting to discover anything I didn't already know. It was more like I wanted to take who I was—who I had become—and remember how that person had been molded by that farm. You know, the lessons my parents drilled into me about hard work and taking responsibility for your actions. The way I learned to work on that farm was the same way I worked when I was in business for myself. And the way my parents taught me to respect other people. That's

> the same way I always tried to show respect for my family and my employees and my neighbors.

For Arthur, the trip provided more reaffirmation than discovery. He explained,

> A lot of things came together. You remember getting up early to find eggs and feed the chickens. And you say to yourself, Yes, that was just like me, even back then. It was just like me to get up each morning with no help from anyone and be responsible for seeing that the work got done. I was maybe no older than seven or eight at the time. When you look back like that, it's like the whole thing—I guess you could say my whole life—just made sense.

Finding Useful Information

All the current-issues participants we placed in the search-for-meaning subgroup called the visit a success. However, none described anything like an epiphany in which everything fell into place and the answers to what they should do with their lives were suddenly apparent. The experience was more like going to a library and locating the information they needed to move forward with a long-standing project. What did they bring home with them? Here are their words:

> A better idea of myself, of the boy I was and the man I became.
>
> An appreciation for how my experiences back then affected me.
>
> Some things I had not thought about in a long time. Things that are important to remember.
>
> A perspective. A viewpoint to go to when I want to look at my life.
>
> Memories. They're like facts. They give you a factual basis to make your judgments with, to know what you really went through as a child and not what you imagine.
>
> A starting point for working through questions about what kind of person I am and what I wanted in life.

Dealing with Current Problems

Psychologists who study life stories often look for transitions—turning points in which lives are changed in significant ways. Sometimes transitions are obvious, such as having a child or moving across the country to accept a promotion. Other times we recognize turning points only in hindsight, such as when a part-time summer job launches a new career or when we meet that friend of a friend at a party—the one who eventually becomes our spouse.

Transitions can also force their way into our lives in the form of a problem or crisis. About half the people we placed in the current-issues category were wrestling with specific problems in their lives when they decided to visit their childhood home. Their problems were similar to the ones most of us face from time to time—relationships, health, employment, family, finances. Most of these participants recognized at the time that they were in a moment of transition. Changing jobs or leaving a relationship is an obvious time for closing some doors and opening others. What makes these individuals different from most people is the strategy they employed. All had a sense that getting back in touch with their childhoods would help. As one participant explained, "Your life is going one way, and then all of a sudden it's not. That's an opportunity. That's when you need to reassess, to figure out what's important and what you're going to do about it." Another participant put it this way: "You have to know where you've been before you know where you're going."

Elise visited her childhood home when she was forty. She had not seen the house since she had left twenty-three years earlier, but she decided it was time her three children saw their grandparents and the other relatives who still lived in the community. So, Elise drove back to the small Indiana town where she had lived from ages four to seventeen.

At the time, she was aware of a general dissatisfaction with her life and had a vague feeling that her emotional restlessness might be related to the trip. "[It was] the year before I got a divorce, and I was kind of like getting my life together," she said. "I knew I had to do something. And I went back and visited. In a way—not consciously, but subconsciously—I think it was a way of checking out where I had been. Because at that point in time, I wasn't quite certain where I was going." It was only in hindsight that Elise recognized the real reason for her visit. "I thought in the back of my mind that I might file for a divorce from my husband," she said. "But I wasn't quite sure. I was toying with the idea. And then a year later, I did. So it was a part of that whole thing. Sort of checking out where I've been."

Elise spoke to us when she was sixty-three, more than two decades after her divorce. Piecing the connections together years later, she saw a clear link between the visit and her decision to leave her husband. "What I didn't realize until that trip was that I had a childlike relationship with my husband," she said. While showing her children her old home and neighborhood, Elise came to appreciate how much she had grown and changed over the years. In contrast, her relationship with her husband seemed stuck in an earlier, less mature place. She had fallen into a pattern of accepting his verbal abuse, she concluded, as if she were still the submissive girl who lived in that small Indiana town. "That's an insight I'm not sure I would have come to without the visit," she said.

Alberto knew just what his problem was when he visited his childhood home. He was thirty-six at the time and about to lose his job. Being laid off is rarely good news, but in Alberto's case the impending unemployment held a deeper meaning. He had left home with big ambitions, certain that by the time he reached his mid-thirties, he would be a huge financial success. But things had not turned out as planned, and his looming job loss forced Alberto to face the sad fact that he had fallen far short of his dreams. It seemed like a good time to reassess.

Alberto made his first and only trip back to the Phoenix housing projects where he had grown up. "I just went back home and tried to remember what had happened when I was a kid," he said. "And I tried to figure out why I hadn't achieved any more than I had." His family and friends had all moved away in the twenty-one years since he had seen the place. But he found the old buildings where he had grown up, and, predictably, the memories came back. However, the insights he gained were not pleasant. As Alberto walked around his old neighborhood, he became keenly aware of "how backward, naive, and inexperienced I was when I was a kid." Looking at his childhood home through adult eyes, he appreciated for the first time how truly disadvantaged he had been when he started out in life. Growing up in a poor home with uneducated parents had not prepared him to get ahead in the world. "I used to do real good in school," he recalled. "I had good teachers. They expected a lot from you. And being a kid, I didn't know any better. I thought, 'I'm going to go out and grab the bull by the horns.' And then you grow up and find out things aren't as easy as they look."

After a couple of hours, Alberto got back in his car and drove home. Over the next few days, he came to see that becoming a financial success had never really been his goal in life. It had been imposed on him by family and friends. That insight freed Alberto from the expectations that had driven his career choices to that point, and he started considering for the first time just what kind of career he really wanted.

Mortality, Symbols, and Spirituality

One woman called the day after her interview to tell me about an image from her trip that had come to her the previous night. Linda wasn't sure why, but she wanted to tell me about the farmhouses scattered around the fields near the area where she had grown up. During her visit, she discovered that nearly all the farms had been abandoned. Structures that once were homes to farmers and their families sat empty and boarded up. "They were just shells sitting there," she said. "They didn't have any paint on them. They didn't have any windows. I remembered them as fine working farms. But now they looked like they were just sitting there, that nobody was tending them."

A sadness came into Linda's voice as she thought about the empty farmhouses. "It was weird because I didn't know what had happened to the neighbors," she said. "Had they died? Had they just moved away? It was just sort of a sad and strange feeling that I can't really explain, except that maybe I never thought those farms would die off and just sit there like empty shells. It just seemed like something that never should have happened." She paused in a moment of self-reflection before continuing. "I don't know, maybe they just reminded me of my own mortality."

Like Linda, several participants saw a connection between their visit to a childhood home and their mortality. Perhaps such questions are inevitable when reflecting on the course of one's life. Here are how some of our participants described the experience:

> Seeing how things were when I was a child made me realize just how fast time was slipping away from me. You know, when you're a kid, time isn't an issue. You have the sense that life will go on forever. And I guess I had avoided really thinking about it very much. But that day, I started to really feel that life was short.

> At that point I was around forty-two, and when you approach that age you have more of a feeling of your own mortality and your own limitations. It was kind of a midlife crisis to a certain extent.

> When you reach a certain age, you think about death. That's just natural. And that gets you thinking about your life. And you want to get in touch with that life, to reassure yourself about certain parts of it. That it was real. That it was good. So you want to go back to the old neighborhood really just to reassure yourself that it was a good life, a life worth living.

Although thoughts about death can easily become morbid and sad, this was not the case for the participants who expressed a concern about mortality during our interviews. In one way or another, each talked about the satisfaction they felt in seeing that something from their past not only had survived but also was likely to be there long after they were gone. "As long as the place is still there, I feel like my childhood is still alive somehow," one woman said. "It's like when people talk about wanting to leave something behind, leave some mark they made on the world. Life is so fleeting. I know my childhood is gone. But when I saw the house and the yard and the evergreen trees, I had the feeling that my childhood still existed somehow."

The connection between mortality concerns and connecting with one's childhood can be partially understood if we think about places as an extension of the self-concept. As described in earlier chapters, people often include their childhood home as part of their personal identity. One man put it this way: "The house was part of who I was. If the old house hadn't been there, then it would have been like losing an arm or a leg."

We might say that childhood homes are symbols of one's life, or at least the life one had as a child. If that is the case, then seeing the house standing and looking like it did decades before can be reaffirming. This way of thinking also helps us understand the reactions of people who feel as if some important part of themselves has been destroyed when they discover that the buildings from their childhood are gone.

We can see another example of homes as symbols when we look at the way communities treat the childhood homes of famous people. All across this country, and in many other nations, former homes of leaders, performers, writers, and artists have been restored and preserved. Many have been turned into museums, and I confess that I have occasionally gone quite a few miles out of my way to see the childhood home of a deceased writer or artist whose work I admire. No doubt there is something to be learned in seeing the physical place where Mark Twain or Georgia O'Keeffe grew up. We can speculate about what the person's life must have been like and how those experiences might have shaped his or her work. But in truth, people probably visit former homes of famous individuals because the homes are physical representations of the person. To visit Graceland is to visit Elvis.

Exactly which famous homes to preserve and which to destroy can be a source of heated debate. For many years, Seattle residents and city officials battled over what to do with a small, dilapidated two-bedroom house in a run-down neighborhood.[5] The building was a hangout for vagabonds and drug addicts, and the city wanted it torn down. But the house also had been the childhood home of legendary rock and blues guitarist Jimi Hendrix. Was that reason enough to keep the building standing? An eventual compromise moved the house to a lot in nearby Renton, Washington, across the street from the cemetery where Hendrix is buried. About the same time, a Liverpool city council committee voted to demolish a childhood home of former Beatles drummer Ringo Starr, even though the city had already taken steps to preserve the childhood homes of fellow Beatles John Lennon and Paul McCartney.[6] The committee explained that Ringo had lived in that particular house for only three months, whereas John and Paul had spent a significant part of their lives in the preserved sites.

Battles over what to do with places associated with famous people are not limited to former homes. Recently, Baltimore wrestled with the question of what to do about the old buildings and grounds that comprise Cardinal Gibbons School. In the first half of the twentieth century, the structures were known as St. Mary's Industrial School for Boys, part orphanage and part reform school. From age seven to nineteen, an "incorrigible" George Herman ("Babe") Ruth spent a good part of this life there. Although it was not exactly a former home, there Ruth discovered baseball and developed into the larger-than-life personality who became an American icon. To those who want to preserve the school, something important would be lost if the structure and grounds were destroyed. "He [Ruth] learned the game on that soil," said Michael Gibbons, director of the Babe Ruth Birthplace and Museum. "You can touch it. It's tangible."[7]

Many of the people we interviewed talked about mortality and finding meaning in their lives. Surprisingly, they didn't talk about religion. Indeed, only a handful of participants even mentioned the subject. And although a few visited churches during their trips, no one made the church or religious concerns a major focus of the visit. Out of all the people we interviewed, only one said she had discussed her trip with a member of the clergy.

This observation may say something about the kind of people who answered our ad or the kind of people who live in my part of the country. But I suspect the absence of religion in these conversations may also reflect a larger societal trend. Although religion remains an important part of many Americans' lives, a large number of people today seek to satisfy their spiritual needs through avenues outside of traditional churches.[8] A recent survey found that more Americans describe themselves as "spiritual" than "religious."[9] If we define the term broadly, spirituality seems to be what many of our participants were talking about when they discussed the reasons for their trips. Visiting their childhood homes formed one step in a larger quest to understand their lives and find meaning in their existences. Whether one sees this as a "religious" or a "spiritual" journey may simply be a matter of definition. At least for the people we spoke with, however, traditional organized religions did not seem to play a significant role in their experiences.

Case Study: Catherine

One August day when she was thirty-five, Catherine made an impulsive decision to drive from California to her childhood home in Billings, Montana. She was recently divorced and suddenly hounded by questions about the direction her life was taking.

"I was doing some self-exploration," she said, "really trying to figure out where I wanted to go in life. I was thirty-five, and I had a couple of kids, and really kind of didn't know what I wanted to do with my life and where I wanted to go. My kids had gone to summer camp. And I just decided to take this trip."

Catherine grew up in a rural house her father built when she was four. She no longer had relatives in Billings and had not been back since her family moved to Oregon when she was fourteen. In the twenty-one intervening years, she had never seriously considered a return trip.

"I decided to drive, taking roads I had never driven before," she said. "I turned off my radio and took off my watch. And I kept a journal. I didn't have an itinerary, so I didn't know where I was going to stay or when."

Why did she make the trip? Catherine was forty-seven when we spoke with her. In hindsight, she thought she understood what had been going on at the time. "I asked myself," she said, "what can I do? What do I want from my life? What's important to me? How can I live on my own? It was really self-exploration. Going back. Looking around at my roots. Seeing what was there."

The first place she visited was the house. From a distance, it looked much the same as she remembered, except that the trees had grown considerably. She parked her car and walked down the dirt road that led to her former home. She said,

> There was a swing set my dad had put in cement in the ground, and it was still there. I stood there and looked and looked. But I didn't have what it took to knock on the door. Then I walked the route I had taken to grade school. I collected pinecones from the tree that my dad had planted. I ended up giving them to my sister. I thought I would keep them, but when she found out I had them, she said, "Oh, I want those." She has never been back, so I gave her the pinecones.

Catherine also visited her elementary and junior high school, her best friend's house, her church, the caves she used to play in, and some rocks she used to climb. She took lots of pictures. After three days, she was ready to leave. What did she gain from the visit? One unexpected benefit had to do with her daughter. At the time of her trip, Catherine's oldest daughter was fourteen, the same age Catherine had been when she last lived in Montana. As memories of those earlier days came to her, the connection with her daughter was unavoidable. "I could clearly remember what I was like when I was fourteen," she said. "And it put [my daughter's] life in perspective. I became a much gentler mother. I became much more empathetic to what it's like to be fourteen."

But the larger benefit was the one she had been seeking when she impulsively jumped into her car and took off her watch. Catherine had come to Montana with no particular plan but wisely allowed a lot of time for reflection. "I spent some time on the trip with my journal," she said, "looking at relationships in my life and putting them in perspective and thinking about them. Especially my relationship with myself."

Catherine took a long look at herself, and she liked what she saw. "I realized how strong I was," she said. "From that point on, I felt much more in control of my life. I remember driving home, coming into the valley on [Highway] 680 and just being so excited. It was the first time I'd really felt like that. I had so many ideas of things I wanted to do."

CHAPTER SIX

~

A Place to Heal

Several years ago, documentary filmmaker Andrew Jarecki was working on a movie about David Friedman, a man who made his living performing as a clown at children's parties. As Jarecki probed Friedman for background information, he became suspicious about his subject's responses. "The stories he was telling me about his family were these kind of neatly packaged stories that didn't really go anywhere," Jarecki explained. "And knowing what I know about families and how screwed up they often are, it seemed to me implausible."[1]

And so Jarecki tried something else:

> I said to him, "Why don't we go back to your house where you were a kid?" And he said, "No, we don't really need to do that." And I said, "No, no, let's do that." And so we went back, and I seated him on the steps of his boyhood home, and he gives me sort of this same routine for a while. And I said, "That's really it?" And he said, "Yeah, that's pretty much it. My father was a great guy, and my mother was crazy, and my brothers were wonderful." And I said, "When was the last time you were in your bedroom?" And he said, "Oh, it's been many, many years." So I went up, and I knocked on the door, and there was a woman that owns the house now, and she let him go into his bedroom. And I stayed outside for the time that he was in his bedroom. And finally, by the time he came out, he was a little wobbly, a little emotional. And it was the first time I'd seen him like that. And he sat back down, and I said, "All right, is there anything else you want to tell me?" And he said, "No, no, that's pretty much it. Unless you want to hear about my mom's suicide attempt."[2]

This revelation was Jarecki's first clue that, as he suspected, there was more to Friedman's tale than met the eye. Additional probing and a lot more research led the filmmaker to the story of a family torn apart years earlier by accusations of child molestation, a father who eventually took his own life in prison, and a brother who spent thirteen years behind bars for a crime he almost certainly did not commit. What became the highly acclaimed film *Capturing the Friedmans* might never have been made if Jarecki had not taken advantage of the powerful reaction people often have when visiting a childhood home. In this case, the unfortunate and tragic nature of the events that took place in that home amplified the emotional response. Jarecki explained his insight this way: "I just thought that the closer I got him to his childhood physically, the more likely he was going to be there emotionally."[3]

Like for David Friedman, some people's childhood homes are storerooms for dark and painful memories. Returning to those homes can evoke disturbing recollections at least as powerful as the pleasant ones reported by participants in earlier chapters. I placed 12 percent of the participants in my study into the unfinished-business category. Each of these individuals had a childhood marred by sad or tragic experiences. In some cases, the painful experience was a single event, such as the death of a parent. For other participants, mistreatment and abuse characterized much of their childhood. Most of these individuals moved away from their childhood homes and surrounding communities as soon as they were legally and financially able. Yet, all discovered years later that they had not succeeded in putting the past behind them. Many experienced symptoms typically found in people suffering from exposure to trauma: depression, anxiety, relationship problems. Others felt incomplete or that something important was missing from their lives. Eventually, they all decided to return physically to the starting point of their troubles. None expected their visits to be pleasant. But each felt making the trip was something he or she had to do.

I found participants in the unfinished-business category could be roughly divided into two groups, although in a few cases individuals had gone through both kinds of experiences. One group described unhappy childhoods that often included trauma or abuse. The other group had their childhoods interrupted by the death of a parent.

Unhappy Childhoods

People often describe childhood as a special time of life, characterized by innocence and the joy of daily discoveries. We picture smiling girls and boys on playground equipment and toddlers securely nestled in their parents' arms. Unfortunately, as psychologists have known for some time, too many children are raised in less-than-ideal circumstances. An estimated one in four children in this country grows up in a home where one or both parents have an alcohol problem.[4] Alcoholic homes can be chaotic and stressful for children. Which Dad will come home tonight, the one who hugs or the one who screams and hits? Conflict and hostility are common in these families. Children learn to fend for themselves, to suffer through the yelling and fighting, and to hide their family secret from their friends. Studies find a host of problems among people psychologists refer to as adult children of alcoholics. These problems include relationship difficulties, anxiety disorders, substance abuse, and physical health issues.[5]

But unhappy childhoods are not limited to homes with a substance-abusing parent. A study by the U.S. Department of Health and Human Services estimated that more than nine hundred thousand American children suffer from physical, emotional, or sexual abuse each year, largely at the hands of their parents.[6] The potential long-term consequences of this abuse are numerous. The list includes brain damage, chronic diseases, learning disabilities, juvenile delinquency, substance abuse, and academic problems.[7] One study estimated that as many as 80 percent of abused children will meet the diagnostic criteria for one or more psychological disorders in adulthood.[8] Depression and anxiety are among the most common symptoms.

Children also can be subjected to abuse and humiliation outside the home. In one survey of students in grades six through twelve, one in five said they had been hit, slapped, or kicked by a bully during school hours,[9] and 25 percent said they were afraid another student was going to hit them. Other studies find that as many as half of all school children are bullied at some time before they graduate from high school, and at least 10 percent are bullied on a regular basis.[10] The result of all this abuse from classmates can be severe. Each year approximately 160,000 students nationwide miss some school time out of fear of being bullied.[11] Although many bullying incidents are quickly dismissed and forgotten, psychologists recognize the long-term damage to self-esteem and emotional stability that often results from bullying, particularly if the victimization is ongoing. In the most extreme cases, children have refused to leave the house and have even committed suicide.[12]

In short, childhood is not always sweet and happy. People who suffer through abusive childhoods develop a number of strategies for coping with their experiences. Remarkably, some survive the trauma with few, if any, noticeable effects. But many continue to suffer. Psychologists' offices are filled with these people. And we learned from our interviews that some of these individuals employ a paradoxical strategy for dealing with their painful pasts: they return to the place where many of their troubles started.

Returning to an Abusive Home

At first glance, we might think that people who grew up in abusive families would be the least likely candidates to visit a childhood home. What advantage is there to releasing the torrent of memories and emotions that inevitably come with such a trip? No doubt the experience would be overwhelming and perhaps counterproductive for many individuals. But if the idea is to obtain a better idea of what happened and to work through the emotions associated with the experience, then surrounding oneself with visual and other sensory cues might be a powerful therapeutic tool.

Most of the unfinished-business participants who grew up in abusive homes were seeing a professional counselor at the time of their visit or did so shortly after the trip. This is probably advisable. Simply visiting a childhood home is unlikely to resolve lifelong issues by itself. Rather, returning to the place where the abuse occurred is probably best viewed as one step in a longer therapeutic process.

What can be gained by returning to the scenes of sadness and trauma? One of the most consistent findings from research with trauma victims is that the painful experience must be acknowledged and dealt with.[13] Although no single therapeutic plan works for everyone, psychologists often find that talking or even writing about a traumatic event can go a long way toward helping one cope with the experience and its psychological and physical toll. Consider the procedure developed by psychologist James Pennebaker and his colleagues.[14] Participants in these studies were asked to identify a traumatic or emotionally painful experience from their past that they had told few or no people about. One of the amazing findings from this research is how readily most people can identify such an experience. Next participants are asked to write about the experience and the emotions surrounding it. Typically, participants write for fifteen minutes on four consecutive days. Another group of participants is instructed to write for the same amount of time on a series of unemotional topics (such as a description of their living room). Then the researchers wait—usually for several months—before taking measures of psychological and physical health in both groups.

Can sixty minutes of writing about a traumatic experience—sometimes an event that has haunted a person for decades—have substantial long-term benefits? A series of studies suggests that it can.[15] Participants writing about unsettling events typically experienced an increase in stress immediately after reliving the trauma on paper. But several months later, these individuals tended to show better emotional adjustment than those who wrote about trivial topics. Moreover, measures of health—such as absences from school or work and number of visits to a doctor—indicate that putting one's emotions into words also has physical benefits. In short, dealing with the experience directly rather than avoiding it can bring one a long way toward recovery.

Many of our participants had a similar insight. Prior to their visits, most had tried to cope with their emotional scars through various methods of avoidance. Most had spoken to few people about the abuse they suffered, and in no case had they gone back to see the old home and neighborhood until they felt it was time to do so. One woman made a point of keeping no photographs, toys, or other memorabilia from her painful childhood. When a relative sent her some old black-and-white snapshots of her parents, she tore them up and threw them away.

Eventually, the people we spoke with all came to see what psychologists have found repeatedly in their studies: in the long-run, these types of avoidance strategies are rarely, if ever, effective.[16] Although many came to this understanding with the help of a professional counselor, most made the decision to visit their childhood home on their own. A few described the decision this way:

> When I heard that mother had died, I knew I had reached an important point in my life. What I had been running away from—what I had been trying to put behind me—was still there, and it wasn't going to go away without me doing something about it.

> You can pretend that what's past is past, but deep down inside I think you know that it really isn't so. I had to go back to that house to see for myself. To see if what I was remembering was true. Going back there was the only way really to determine if this thing was as big as I thought, or if I had somehow let it take more control over me than I should have.

Janice was forty-seven when we interviewed her. She did not remember large blocks of time from her childhood, but what she could recall was not pleasant. She grew up in a military complex in South Dakota where she suffered physical and emotional abuse at the hands of her parents. She also was sexually abused. One thing Janice clearly remembers is her mother's obsession with waxing and polishing the hardwood floors—the floors on which Janice was often beaten. To this day, she cannot stand the smell of furniture polish.

Janice left that home when she went off to college at eighteen and had planned to stay away forever. More than twenty years later, she and her husband were driving through South Dakota about an hour away from the military complex. She still cannot remember what she was doing in that part of the country or how she made the decision to see her former home. But she was pleased to discover that the complex was closed. Many of the buildings had been torn down, and the rest sat empty. "I was able to go there because there was nothing there anymore," she said. "But I had to do it. If it wasn't at that point, I would have done it at another time in my life. I needed to get closure."

One of the two houses she had lived in was still standing. She peeked through a window into the empty building and was surprised by her reaction. "I saw the house as it used to be, with the furniture, with the curtains, with the plants, but no people. I saw the way it used to look. And the smell. I could smell the waxed floors, the hardwood floors and the wax my mother used on them."

The visit, combined with extensive psychological counseling, helped Janice work through the residue of her painful childhood. "When I first left, I was very anxious to leave," she said. "Now, as an adult . . . I am able to say goodbye to childhood memories, to say goodbye to an unhappy life. I had to grieve for that loss and then go on to the next stage of my life. It was hard. It took me a long time to get over that."

Of all the interviews I conducted during my research, the one with Annie touched me the most. Annie had few positive memories of her childhood. Her mother, an alcoholic, was mentally and physically abusive. Although she did not want to go into detail, Annie said only that her experience was similar to that of Sybil, the famous multiple-personality case. So, when she was seventeen, Annie eagerly left her hometown—a small, Midwestern farming community—to attend college. Eventually she made her way to the West Coast and never set foot anywhere near her former home until her mother's death twenty years later. Annie made the trip for the funeral. She could have simply attended the services and gotten back on the plane. But there was something else she felt she had to do.

"I wanted to validate my experiences," she said. "To see how I feel about it now. To put my feelings more in perspective. Now that I'm older and no longer in that alcoholic family, I wanted to take the power out of those memories."

So, after the funeral, Annie went by herself to the house. Although two decades had passed and her mother was dead, she still found the experience frightening. As she spoke, I could see in her face and hear in her voice that she was reliving the experience:

> I remember feeling very eerie. This was an awful place to be. I felt a lot like I did when I lived in this house. I actually felt scared. Like I should get out of here. Almost as if something might be recreated. The memories are so terrible. There were some really awful things that happened there. Of course, she was dead and gone at that time, but it was almost as if she could come back while I'm here and get me. The feeling was real strong. Like this is not a good place for me to be—let's get out of here. Because I wanted out of there all the time I lived there. I wanted out of there, but I couldn't leave because I wasn't old enough to take care of myself. It was a really strange feeling, like all these terrible things happened here and you don't want to be here. This is not a place for you to be.

Annie ran out of the house and never returned. Although many years had passed when I spoke with her, reliving the experience during the interview was very difficult. She paused several times to cry and then compose herself.

A few years after her one and only visit to her childhood home, Annie's brother called to say that he had obtained legal ownership of the house. Best of all, he told her, he had hired some professionals to destroy what remained of the structure and have it removed. The news elated Annie. The place that harbored so much fear was gone. But destroying the place was not enough.

"It deserves more," she told me.

"Like what?" I asked.

"More flattening. I know. Fill it in with flowers. Flatten it, get rid of everything, and fill it with flowers."

"Why flowers?" I asked.

"To make it pretty." She started to cry. "What else could you do with it? To take something like that . . . " More tears. "To make it pretty. What else could you do with it?"

Is returning to a former home an effective method for dealing with the aftermath of childhood trauma? I have only a handful of cases to draw conclusions from, but the participants who tried it generally report mixed success. No one regretted the decision to make the trip, but visiting the home proved to be more difficult than a few had imagined. Some participants felt they benefitted from reviving memories that then became the focus of subsequent therapy sessions. Others were less sure if the benefits outweighed the emotional toll. There was general agreement among these participants that people in their situation should make the trip only when they felt they were ready. In short, visiting a home that was once the site of childhood trauma can be a powerful experience. It's a step that should be taken with care.

The Need to Grieve

Loss and bereavement are an unavoidable part of life. Most Western cultures grant individuals a period for grieving following the loss of a loved one. Indeed, we expect people to openly express sorrow, forego pleasant activities, and go through a process of "working through" their grief. We also expect the process to be completed within a reasonable period and that the person will be "over" the experience a year or two after the death. However, psychologists find that each of us responds differently to the loss of a loved one.[17] In particular, whereas some people return to a normal pattern of activity and emotion within a short period, others may take decades to feel that they are truly over the loss.

Several participants we placed in the unfinished-business category had suffered the loss of a parent while they were growing up. Although all of these individuals were decades past the experience when we spoke with them, adults in this situation often have not reached full closure in the bereavement process. Studies find that grieving is very different for children than for adults. Children under twelve in particular have difficulty identifying and expressing their emotions.[18] The process is complicated when adults communicate directly or indirectly that the emotions the child is experiencing are inappropriate. Indeed, young children may not fully appreciate the finality of death, and none are able to appreciate the impact a parent's absence will have on their lives.

Because the grieving they experienced as a child was insufficient, some adults go through what psychologists call regrieving.[19] That is, although many years have passed, these individuals allow themselves to experience a sense of loss and to work through the emotions as if the parent had only recently passed away. Several of our participants more or less described this experience. As part of the regrieving process, they returned to a former home and immersed themselves in a sea of relevant memories and emotions. At that point, the grieving they had been unable to experience as a child was able to proceed.

Many of these individuals included in their trip a visit to the cemetery where their parents were buried. Among all the people we interviewed, only 12 percent visited a cemetery. In most cases, the participants who sought out a parent's grave simply wanted to pay their respects. But participants in the unfinished-business category talked about something more. They allowed thoughts and emotions to rise to the surface. Many spoke aloud as they stood alone in the cemetery, expressing feelings they had been too young to give voice to earlier. Here are their words:

A child doesn't have a real good idea of what death is. For me, I didn't even appreciate how my mother's passing affected me until years later. How could I? You have to be more mature; you have to have a perspective from which to understand such things. But the time came when I needed to revisit that. I had to say some things to my father, to stand there next to his headstone and say them out loud.

I think a lot of people deal with the death of a parent in steps, a little at a time. But there comes a day when you have to finish the grieving. I knew I was ready to do that. So I looked forward to just being there, kind of making my peace with the whole situation.

Glenda's mother died unexpectedly at the age of thirty-seven, when Glenda was only twelve years old. Her father, left to raise five children, was not one to show emotion. He never openly grieved the loss of his wife, and he communicated to the children that they should follow his example. "To him, it was stiff upper lip," Glenda said. "We're not going to fall apart here. Just get on with things. Get busy and get going. It's okay to cry, but do it in your room." As a result, none of the children were allowed to work through the emotional loss and their feelings of abandonment.

Glenda had visited the house from her New England childhood only a few weeks before we talked with her. The decision to make the trip was triggered by a confluence of several events. One was the twenty-fifth anniversary of her mother's death. Not coincidentally, Glenda also had just turned thirty-seven, the same age her mother was when she died. But what finally pushed Glenda to make the trip was a discussion with a friend about emotional bonds between mothers and their children. In a moment of insight, Glenda realized that she had been holding back emotionally from her own children. She also realized that she feared dying young and putting her children through the emotional pain she still carried from her mother's death. Her failure to work through the loss was keeping Glenda from getting close to her own children.

And so she made the trip. She saw the old house and walked the halls of her old school. She retraced the route she used to take when delivering newspapers as a child. But the most important stop was the one she made at the cemetery where her mother was buried. "I expected I would be crying buckets and be emotionally overwhelmed," she said. "But I wasn't at all. It was actually rather peaceful."

Glenda had planned what she would say and do, but the experience unfolded differently than she had anticipated. "I kind of cleaned up around my mother's grave," she said. "I had pictured this out-loud conversation and saying good-bye. But I couldn't do it. It wasn't because I was sitting there crying. It was that I didn't need to anymore. I just sat there and felt real peaceful about it." When we interviewed Glenda, she was working with her minister on accepting her mother's death and being emotionally available to her children.

All the unfinished-business participants who visited their childhood home as part of a regrieving process found the experience valuable. It is probably safe to say that each of them had reached a point at which they were emotionally ready for the experience. Visiting the childhood home formed but one step in a longer process of coming to grips with the parent's death. However, it is worth mentioning that taking this step may not be for everyone going through regrieving. Moreover, visiting a childhood home is not likely to be helpful until the individual feels the timing is right.

Case Study: Andrea

Until she was sixteen, Andrea lived in what many would consider a dreamworld. Her father was in the motion picture business, and her childhood home was an elegant mansion in Southern California. Andrea remembers her mother's walk-in closet with rows of evening gowns for the frequent awards ceremonies and Hollywood social gatherings. Andrea had just about everything a child could want. And then her father died.

From the day of her father's death, Andrea's life changed dramatically: no more glamorous lifestyle, no more mansion. The adjustment was too much for a teenager. She turned to alcohol and then to drugs. By the time she reached twenty, Andrea was a heavy user and abuser of both. She would struggle with this problem for the next twenty years.

Although she often lived within easy driving distance of her childhood home, Andrea did not see the house again until she was nearly forty. Then one day, as she was driving nearby with a man with whom she was romantically involved, she felt a strong desire to see the house again. "It was very compelling," she said. "It's hard to explain. There was a driving force there. Every time I drove near there, it probably was in the back of my mind. To go in[side the house]. But it just seemed rather uncivilized to impose upon people. But this time I had somebody I looked up to [with me], and I wanted him to understand a little about where I came from."

Andrea rang the doorbell and explained to the maid who answered that she had grown up in the house. The owners were not home, but to her surprise, the maid allowed Andrea and her companion to look around inside.

The experience was overwhelming. Memories of "parties and people" came flooding back. She recalled the furniture and the paintings. But most of all, she thought about her father's death. "It was kind of like passing the scene of an accident," she said. "A lot of anxiety set in. And grieving. A lot of grieving. I don't deal with grieving, so when there's a loss—whether it be a person, or a way of life, or a home—I tend to find things to replace it. But I don't deal with it at all."

They stayed about forty-five minutes. Over the next few days, Andrea could talk about nothing else except the house. "It was hard to get my mind off it," she said. "I would run through the rooms in the house. It was like I had my business and my relationship and everything, but a certain percentage of my thoughts were on the house. It was like a little private room in my head where I was just hanging onto a lot of stuff." Then she fell into a depression that lasted several months. Andrea knew her depression had something to do with her visit to her former home. She tried writing exercises, mentally going through the house and writing down her feelings about each room.

Later that year, her family gathered for a funeral of a distant relative. After the service, Andrea suggested to her mother and sister that the three of them visit the old house. They called the owners and found them more than agreeable. "The people understood the impact the house had upon us, and they left us alone," Andrea said. "We ended up staying three or four hours. We all went off in different directions. I was comfortable enough that I could sit in one spot and just stare at something. I had time to absorb things."

The second trip turned out to be the beginning of the grieving process Andrea had never allowed herself. She explained,

> I learned that I had a lot of anger. Anger about my father dying and the family unit changing. I always had a feeling that my childhood life was going to be the way it was. I just never considered that it could be any different. And when it did become different, I never accepted it. I started drinking alcohol and using drugs. That was always a pretty handy device for me not to carry feelings all the way through. It was a lot easier for me to deal with it that way.

We interviewed Andrea two years after her second visit to the house. She was forty-two years old at the time and had been in a substance-abuse recovery program for six months.

CHAPTER SEVEN

When There's No Place Like Home

Over the years, I have presented my work on visiting childhood homes to various groups. Although the presentations always include time for questions, inevitably a few people linger about after the talk, hoping for an extended conversation. Many want to share their own experiences about a visit to their childhood home. Some want advice for an upcoming trip. But it is not uncommon for someone with a very different perspective also to hang around. After others have chatted and gone, this person politely asks some variation of the question, What about me?

These aren't people whose reasons for visiting a childhood home don't fit into any of my three categories. Nor are they individuals who simply lack a desire to reconnect with a home they lived in during their elementary school years. Rather, these are people who have no specific home with which to reconnect. More accurately, they have too many childhood homes to make any one stand out as special. When I ask audiences to consider a single place from childhood that they think of as their "home," these individuals simply don't know what to think.

Although most Americans have memories of a specific place they lived in during an extended part of their childhood, there are many exceptions to this rule. Many children grow up in circumstances that are not so stable. Sometimes their parents' jobs require frequent moving. Promotions and company relocations often mean a new address. Other children are caught in the pattern of frequent moves that sometimes accompanies poverty. Parents' divorces and new marriages often translate into new neighborhoods, new towns, and new schools for the kids. Some children grow up in unfortunate family situations in which they are shuttled between parents, relatives, and sometimes foster homes. They might spend six months here, twelve months there, and then go to a different place in the summer.

Of particular note are the many children who grow up in families in which one parent, usually the father, has chosen a military career. Children raised in these circumstances often refer to themselves as "military brats." For a number of reasons, military brats have very different experiences than most children. Among the most important of these differences is that military families typically move a lot. Author Mary Edwards Wertsch, herself a military brat, interviewed eighty adults who grew up in military families.[1] The average person in her study had attended 9.5 different schools from kindergarten through high school (the total number of moves was even higher). The toll this frequent moving takes on children can be substantial. Many of Wertsch's participants talked about their inability to develop intimate friendships. Others dealt with the difficulty of being separated from their friends by developing a resistance to attachments. If you keep your classmates at an emotional arm's length, you can avoid the pain that comes with the inevitable good-bye.

Most important, military brats fail to develop a sense of belonging. As Wertsch explains, they come to dislike one question in particular that they nonetheless frequently face in the never-ending process of meeting new people: "*Where are you from?* Military brats do not relish the 'where from' question and go through life vainly trying to parry it. Some answer 'Nowhere.' Others, 'Everywhere.' . . . [Many say] the last place they've been, or the one they liked most. . . . The fact is, there is no way to answer the question [that] is not awkward."

Researchers have only recently begun to look at the psychological effects of feeling rootless. But those who experience it do not like the sensation. Wertsch identified one interesting way that rootlessness rears its head when she asked her participants where they wanted to be buried. Most people want to be buried in the place they call home. For some, this is the family home, that is, a location where other family members are buried. For others, it is the town where they grew up or spent the bulk of their adult life. But how does someone with no sense of belonging anywhere answer that question? Three-quarters of Wertsch's military brats resolved the issue by saying they wanted to be cremated. Yet, even among those who preferred to be buried, most had no idea where that place might be.

Frequent Movers in My Study

It's difficult to say how long it takes to develop an attachment to a home or to incorporate that home into your self-concept. But most likely, the process requires many years. People need time to have the arguments, the intimate moments, the special occasions, the secluded afternoons, and all the other experiences that turn a house into a home. When investigating people who had visited a childhood home, I sought out individuals who could identify a single place from their childhood that they had wanted to see. Naturally, I did not expect very many, if any, of my participants to have moved frequently during their childhood. Nonetheless, when we asked people to identify the various places they had resided during their lives, we found eleven individuals who had lived in ten or more homes before reaching their eighteenth birthday. A few participants had lived in so many places that they could only guess at the actual number. One man thought it was eighteen. Another was sure it was more than twenty. One woman believed she had never lived in one place for more than a year.

Despite this instability, each of these individuals had made a trip specifically to see a childhood home. This finding raised the obvious question, Why would people want to visit a home they had lived in for only a year or, in some cases, even less time? My initial thought was that these participants would have a very different experience than those who had lived in one place for many years. I imagined that their attachment to a former home would not be as strong as it is for most people and that the visit would not be as emotional or as satisfying. As it turns out, I was partly correct and partly incorrect in my assumptions. The stories from the frequent movers were different, but they were no less emotional. And many of these individuals found the experience quite rewarding, although often for different reasons.

Why This Home?

During our interviews, we routinely asked participants why they had chosen this particular place to visit out of all the places they had lived. The answer from most participants was fairly predictable. It was a place they had lived in a long time, and it was a place from their elementary school years. But this was obviously not the case for the participants who had moved frequently during those years. Some of these frequent movers acknowledged that their choice was simply a matter of convenience. They wanted to see a childhood home, and the one they visited was geographically closer than any of the others. For these participants, any childhood home was simply representative of the collection of homes they had once lived in.

"I wasn't even sure I was remembering everything just right," one man said. "I think some of the memories I had when I was standing outside that house are things that really happened someplace else. I moved so often, in my mind all those different houses kind of melted into one house. Being there at this one house sort of stood for all of the houses I lived in during that part of my life."

Other participants selected a home they associated with a particularly powerful memory or with which they felt the strongest emotional connection. One woman chose the home she had lived in during the fifth grade because that was her favorite year from childhood:

> I usually had a difficult time making friends. But that year, I had two very close girl friends. We did everything together. We had slumber parties where we talked about everything. We were just at that age where you start to think about things like boys. But you don't know anything, and that's why it's so important to have close friends to talk to. You can explore and learn things together. And I remember thinking that this is what it must be like for other kids. Of course, I had to move the next year. But I learned a lot from those experiences.

Another woman took the opposite approach. She singled out the house that held the darkest memories from her childhood. "There was a corner I had to sit in when I got into trouble," she said. "It was in the kitchen near a room that was a kind of pantry. And I remember it had this horrible smell. I used to have to sit there facing the corner for the longest time, or at least what seemed like a long time to a little girl."

Something to Cling To

Why would someone who moved continually throughout childhood seek out one home to visit from among many? Like others we interviewed, the frequent movers often talked about making a connection with their pasts. A few used the trip to help with a current life crisis or to address unfinished business from their childhoods. But most also described a feeling that something was missing from their early years. They had recognized at an early age that their lives were different from their classmates'. Some pointed out the advantages of moving so frequently. They got to experience different cultures, see interesting places, and develop the art of making new friends. But they also understood that these pluses came with a price. Here are their words:

> Other kids in the neighborhood know things that you don't. You also want to know all the history about what happened there and learn about all the secret places. But after a while you know that it's not even worth the effort to try and find out, because you're just going to move again anyway.
>
> I hear other people talking about a house where their parents still live, and it always sounds nice. It's like they have one house that they think of as their home. It's a place that belongs to them and their families.
>
> I especially start to think about this around the holidays. All those Christmas shows where they have people gathering around the tree, and they do the same traditional things they do every year. Every Christmas I remember was different, because it was in a different place. There's something good about that, the different experiences and all. I had white Christmases and Christmases in the dessert. But I'm kind of jealous of those people who did the same thing every year.

Of course, it is not clear that the participants I spoke with were representative of most people who moved frequently as children. It might be the case that individuals who moved around a lot during childhood rarely have a strong desire to visit a place from the past. But at least some of these frequent movers have this experience. And the stories they told us reinforce the notion that childhood homes often play a significant role in people's lives, even if their time with that home was brief.

So what were these frequent movers searching for? In one way or another, most of them described a need to find—or perhaps create—something they never had. They were looking for stability, a sense of permanence. They wanted a physical place that represented for them everything that they thought of when they thought of home. Some participants explained that they were motivated to visit one of their childhood homes in part because they lacked a single location they could point to when describing where they grew up. One woman explained,

> My childhood was not like other kid's childhoods. When people ask where I'm from, I just tell them, "You name it, I probably lived there." But that's just a cover-up because . . . I don't really feel like I lived anywhere. It really came to a head for me when my children started asking me. They wanted to know about the house I grew up in when I was a girl. I didn't know what to tell them. I really wished at that point that there had been just one house.

Another woman made the connection more directly. "I think I went back to that house in San Diego," she said, "because I wanted to pretend that there was one place that I could call home. If I had a single place, maybe I wouldn't have even wanted to make the trip. Maybe it was because I traveled around so much as a child that I had this feeling that I needed a permanent place. A base, if you will."

Sorting Memories and Contrasting with the Past

The frequent movers' visits to their childhood homes were just as emotional for them as the trips were for other participants. During the interview, many described the joy and excitement that came with small discoveries and rekindling memories. Others talked about sadness or anger. And, like the other participants, a few cried. In all but one case, the frequent movers said the experience was more positive than negative. A few wanted to make the trip again. And several told us they were considering visits to other homes from their childhood. Obviously, for most, the visit was rewarding. But why?

Two reasons for these reactions surfaced during our interviews. First, the experience helped some participants fill in gaps in their memories. Many talked about their childhood as being a blur. Of course, they had numerous childhood memories like everyone else. But because the events they remembered occurred in so many different places, the memories often seemed scattered. For some participants, seeing some of the places from their past somehow made their childhood feel more organized. One man compared the experience to organizing a filing cabinet:

> You have all these things you remember, but if someone asks you where that happened or where this happened, you don't know. If I think about some kid I once knew and a dog I once had, I can't say if the two things happened during the same year or if they happened years apart. So when I went to this old neighborhood, I was able to sort some of that out. It's like I had a file for things that happened when I was in Minnesota. But until I went there, I couldn't tell if a memory belonged in that particular file or not.

Of course, without traveling to all of their former homes, the frequent movers' ability to sort all of their memories into appropriate categories is limited. It probably also is the case that visiting a home you lived in for only a short period is not quite the same as returning to a place you lived in for many years. Our frequent movers would have missed out on the experience of recalling some of the buried memories from other times in their childhood. Without seeing the sprawling maple in the park, you might not remember the time you fell out of the tree and had to be rushed to the emergency room. On the other hand, human memories are embedded in complex cognitive networks. Bringing forth images from one time in our childhood can help us recall events from other periods. Seeing the skating rink where you fell and broke your right arm might remind you of the time you fell out of the maple tree, even if that tree is a thousand miles away.

Second, many of the people who had moved frequently as children wanted to contrast their current life circumstances with their pasts. Although studies find that people who move frequently as children often continue the pattern as adults,[2] this was not the case for any of the participants we interviewed. Several of these individuals were quick to point out that, as adults, they had lived in the same home for a lengthy period. It was as if reminding themselves of the past reinforced some of the decisions they had made as adults. Some participants mentioned that they would never put their children through all the disruptions they had to endure. A few specifically identified themselves as better parents than their own mothers or fathers had been.

That perception certainly seemed to be the case for the woman who visited the home where her mother made her sit in the kitchen corner with the distinct odors. When she first saw the house after more than two decades, she quickly took a walk around the block to gather her thoughts. She had hoped that the place would be abandoned so that she could walk inside. But a family was obviously living there, and she could not bring herself to knock on the door. Eventually she stood across the street for what she thought was about thirty minutes and relived some of the events that had occurred inside the house. She explained,

> I thought I would be angry. I think I wanted to be angry with my mother for the way she raised me. But instead I was just sad. The house look sad, which I think now was appropriate. My childhood was sad. I came away from there feeling a little sorry for myself, but I realized that blaming my mother for everything wouldn't do any good. In a lot of ways, her life was even sadder than mine. She was in a bad marriage and a bad financial situation. I remember thinking that I should be the one feeling sorry for her. I've got a lot more going for me in my life today than she ever had.

The Psychological Consequences of Frequent Moves

A child's world can be severely disrupted when a family moves. For the most part, friends, routines, and the comfort of familiar places are all left behind. The child faces the challenge of getting to know new kids and making new friends, a task that does not come easily to many children. The child also has to adjust to new teachers and perhaps new ways of learning. There may be missed lessons all the other kids in class have learned and academic skills everyone else has acquired. Fitting in socially may be even more difficult. Other children are often leery of the new kid and, at times, even cruel.

What are the psychological consequences of these experiences? At first blush, most of us would say that frequent changes of address are not good for a child. Yet, despite the difficulties they faced, few of our frequent movers were ready to condemn their childhood experiences completely. Many pointed to some of the benefits that come with frequent moving. They spoke of developing character and interpersonal skills. No doubt the experience carries some advantages as well as some disadvantages. Increasingly, however, researchers, counselors, and public health providers recognize that frequent moving in childhood is associated with a large number of psychological issues.

One team of investigators examined data from a large stratified sample of American families.[3] They found that only one in four children between the ages of six and seventeen had never experienced a family move. Thus, most children know what it is like to be the new kid in school. But moving once or twice is very different from moving several times. Of the children in the study, 10 percent had experienced six or more moves during their childhood. When the researchers compared the frequent movers with the children who had moved infrequently or not at all, they found several important differences. The frequent movers were more likely to have repeated a grade in school. These children also exhibited more behavior and adjustment problems than the infrequent movers. The problem behaviors included fighting, truancy, disobedience, and cheating.

Many of the behavior problems associated with frequent moves don't surface until the child reaches the turbulent teenage years. Teenagers with a history of frequent moves are more likely than other students to use drugs and alcohol and to be involved in an unwanted pregnancy.[4] They also are more prone to emotional problems, especially bouts of depression, and are at a higher risk for suicide attempts.

One team of researchers looked at adolescent girls who lived in poverty situations.[5] They divided the girls into those who had moved never, once, twice, or three or more times during the previous five years (one girl had moved ten times). Not surprisingly, the girls who had stayed in the same home the entire five years scored the highest on measures of psychological adjustment. Significantly more problems were found in the girls who had moved even once during this time. And the girls who had moved at least three times within a five-year period had more adjustment problems than those in any of the other groups.

Taken together, the research leaves little doubt that frequent moving during childhood is related to psychological problems in children. But fully understanding this relationship is not as easy as it first appears. The challenge for psychologists is to explain why moving is associated with this array of psychological problems.[6] Researchers working in this area find themselves in the difficult business of trying to explain cause and effect from correlational data. That is, the children who move a lot quite likely lead different lives and are exposed to more sources of stress than children who stay in the same home. A child who changes residences frequently may have one or both parents absent much of the time. In fact, moves are often the result of parental separations or divorces. This observation means that the child may have lived in an unhappy home with preoccupied parents prior to the move. Moreover, children who move frequently are more likely than other children to live in poverty and to have been born to teenage mothers. In short, it is not always clear whether highly mobile children experience more psychological problems because they move a lot or whether the same factors that lead to their residential instability, like poverty and family separations, are the real source of the problem.

Fortunately, researchers have ways to answer these questions. Investigators can account for variables like poverty and number of parents when they analyze their data. And when they eliminate the effect of these other influences, the relationship between moving and psychological adjustment in children becomes clear. Researchers consistently find that the more often a child changes addresses, the greater the likelihood of academic and adjustment problems.[7] After adjusting for other differences between the movers and the nonmovers, one team of researchers found that children who change residences frequently are 77 percent more likely to suffer from multiple behavior problems and 35 percent more likely to be held back a grade in school.[8]

What about moving from home to home increases the likelihood of psychological problems for children? Psychologists point to a number of reasons. There are obvious disruptions to the child's education. Children who move frequently also have less involvement in constructive activities like sports and social clubs. But the most important reasons are probably social. For every age group psychologists study—from infants to the elderly—social contact is an important component of psychological well-being.[9] But close friendships take time to develop. If their family situation is also unsettled, children who move a lot may have no dependable source of social support they can turn to in times of stress.

This observation raises another question. What happens to these children when they grow up? Are there lingering effects from a childhood filled with frequent changes of address? One recent investigation provides an answer.[10] The researchers looked at the childhood experiences and psychological well-being of more than seven thousand adults. The pattern they uncovered was clear. Adults who had moved frequently during childhood tended to have more adjustment problems than adults without this history. More intriguing, the researchers found that frequent movers tended to die at a younger age than people who had residentially stable childhoods.

However, these findings held one important caveat. Participants with outgoing personalities—what psychologists refer to as extraversion—showed none of these psychological or early-mortality problems as a result of frequent childhood moves. The problems were found only among people with an introverted personality. Why might this be the case? Extraverted children are better at making new friends in new situations. They're comfortable in a room full of strange children, know how to strike up a conversation, and don't wait for other kids to approach them. As a result, the disruption that comes with moving to a new town and a new school takes less of a toll on these children than on those with a more introverted bend.

No Place to Call Their Own

In chapter 3, I described two important needs children face during their elementary school years: establishing a sense of personal identity separate from their families and parents and developing a sense of personal mastery over the environment. Children often satisfy these needs by exploring and manipulating their physical worlds. They build forts, tree houses, and other spaces that they call their own. These are places they control, a world separate from the home they share with their families. But establishing this sense of independence and mastery is difficult when children feel they are just passing through.

A couple of the frequent movers we interviewed were aware of this void in their childhoods. One man said, "Even before I got around to learning the neighborhood, it was time to leave. There probably were a lot of great things in some of those places we lived. But I felt like I never really got to know them." One woman who said she never lived in any childhood home for more than eighteen months explained, "It doesn't even feel like I lived there. It's more like I was visiting. When you visit a city, you only see the most obvious things, like the tourist areas. But when you live in a place, you know it in a way that visitors don't. You know all its nooks and crannies."

Exploring the neighborhood and finding those special places takes time. Building a fort or a tree house is less enticing when you know that, in all likelihood, you'll probably be gone in a few months. Even the child's ability to shape her own living space in her image or for her own purposes is limited. As one woman I interviewed explained,

> My mother would never even let me put a nail in my bedroom wall. Like if I wanted to hang up a picture or something. We always rented, and my parents said we had to leave the place the way we found it. It was always there, always understood, that this location was just temporary. I saw how other girls had painted their bedrooms different colors. I asked my mother once if I could paint my room yellow. But, of course, that was out of the question.

It's difficult to pinpoint what, if any, consequences there are to not building your own fort or not being able to paint your own room. Certainly, many children miss out on these experiences and do just fine. Moreover, it is entirely possible that children who move frequently develop a sense of independence and mastery in other ways. Nonetheless, I can't help but think that something is lost when these childhood experiences are taken away. One woman who participated in my special places study put it this way: "Without my little place under the stairs, I would have had a different childhood. Kids need places where they can be themselves, where they feel secure enough to do and think anything they want. I think I might be a different person today if my parents had not let me spend time in my little hideaway like they did."

It may be just a little thing, but not having an opportunity to control your own little piece of the world might be one more strike against children who spend much of their elementary school years moving from home to home.

CHAPTER EIGHT

The Bigger Picture

By most accounts, Melia had a happy childhood and the kind of formal education that most parents would wish for their children. In school, she was every teacher's dream. She was identified as a gifted student in the first grade and participated in all the programs and work that came with the label. "School was the thing I did best," she said, "and I reveled in it. I loved making my teachers and parents happy."

But all this academic excellence at an early age came with a price. "During the summers," she said, "I would have anxiety that a new kid would come to my school and replace me as the top student. I didn't know who I would be, if not for that." Melia went on to a private high school where she continued to receive excellent grades and academic accolades. Then she went off to a private liberal arts university where she felt "a ridiculous drive to get the best grade in the class." It was a goal she often achieved.

Melia is the first to acknowledge that she received what most people would call a privileged education. "My teachers truly cared about me and were dedicated to my success," she said. But after leaving school, she was anything but content. "The problem was, I'd invested seventeen years of my life to achievement in school with the implied promise of 'success' at the other end, and when I arrived there I didn't feel successful. I felt unhappy and constantly stressed out; I felt that whatever I did wouldn't ever be enough."

For several years, Melia could not shake the feeling that her education had failed her. Finally, at age twenty-eight, she decided to do something about it. "I knew instinctively that school is where I lost my way, led astray by a system that encouraged me to keep achieving, to keep pushing myself to the limit, without regard for my health and happiness. School never taught me how to live a happy, balanced, fulfilling life."

And so, Melia quite literally went back to school. Not to a new program at a new school. Rather, she returned to her old schools, the places where her views on education and achievement were formed. Melia spent three months visiting each grade level in the same schools she had attended earlier in her life, from kindergarten to college. And she did not merely walk around the school grounds and peek through classroom windows. With permission from administrators and teachers, she physically returned to her old classrooms and did her best to get in touch with the experiences she had gone through years earlier. At her old elementary school, she spent her days assisting teachers in the classrooms and interacting with the students. In middle school, she shadowed students through each class in their schedules. Her middle school adventures included dressing for PE in the girls' locker room and attending a school dance. Finally, she visited her high school and college alma maters and sat in on various classes. The idea was to take a close look at her education through her adult eyes, knowing now what she wished she had known then. It was part of a yearlong self-discovery process she called "reschooling" herself.[1]

The Bigger Picture

Among the surprises I encountered while studying people who visit childhood homes was how this common behavior had completely escaped the attention of psychologists. Here was an act that millions of Americans have performed and that, for many, is psychologically quite powerful. Certainly many therapists have heard their clients talk about these visits, and the numbers tell us that many psychologists have made such trips themselves. Yet, the research reported in this book is to date the only empirical work I know of on this topic.

But psychology research does not take place in a vacuum. My search to understand why people make these trips and what they get out of them brought me into contact with numerous related concepts and many related research topics. For psychological researchers, learning about related areas almost always contributes to our understanding of the behavior we are focused on. In this chapter, I'll look at a few neighboring concepts I encountered within this larger mosaic. One of those concepts is the kind of self-discovery process that Melia experienced. I'll also look at some recent work on how residential mobility affects us and our worlds in ways most of us don't realize. Finally, I'll bring the discussion of home attachment full circle—from childhood residences to the attachment elderly citizens feel for the place they call home.

Visiting Places As Part of Self-discovery

Melia's reschooling experience came to my attention when she contacted me about visiting one of my classes. This was toward the end of her project, and she wanted to sit in on some of the same classes, taught by the same professors, that she had taken as an undergraduate. As it happened, I was teaching a course in personality that quarter, and Melia had taken my personality course during her senior year. At some point I told her about my work with people who visited childhood homes, and a lengthy conversation followed. Although her focus was different from mine, Melia had also discovered the value of visiting places from the past.

"There's something powerful about physical places," she said. "Memories and emotions live there. You can feel the energy of a place if you pay attention; you can know if the people living there or going to school there are happy."

By returning to former classrooms, Melia came to understand how her educational experiences had transformed her from a creative, happy child into a grade-driven student who placed her self-worth in the hands of those who evaluated her. The visits were followed by months of reflection and writing. In the end, Melia found she could let go of her old desire to achieve for achievement's sake and instead pursue the creative interests that she had abandoned for too long. Whether she could have made this transformation without physically returning to the classroom, we will never know. But Melia is convinced that putting herself in the place where her ideas about education started was critical. Here are her words:

> I don't think I could have pushed the reset button on my life so successfully without having returned to the places of my past. I felt it was necessary to go back in order to move forward. If I hadn't physically gone back to those places, I feel that they'd still have emotional power over me, and they would still haunt my subconscious. I would still feel like the ten-year-old over-achiever who almost killed herself by pleasing everyone. In going back to the place I started, I was able to lay to rest the person I used to be. I was able to envision the person I want to be from now on and work toward becoming that person.

Melia's story illustrates an important point—that visiting places from one's past can be an important tool in many kinds of self-discovery exercises. As we have seen, returning to a childhood home is often an act of self-discovery. But there are many other significant places in our lives besides where we lived during our elementary school years. I've talked to many people who have described other locations that hold a special place in their hearts: their first apartment, the area where they spent their favorite summer, a grandparent's home, college, a wonderful vacation spot, places they have worked. Like a childhood home, any of these locations might be considered a part of a person's self-concept. Beyond this, many places from our past provided the setting for significant events in our lives, some wonderful and some filled with pain.

Several people I interviewed about their childhood home understood that they stood to gain something from visiting other significant places from their past. Some combined their visit with stops at other special locations. These side trips included summer camps, relatives' homes, vacation destinations, and other homes they had lived in. As with their visit to the childhood home, seeing these other places often led to a rush of memories and emotions and to the occasional insight.

Several participants who were wrestling with relationship issues found it useful to visit places they associated with their partners. Destinations included the place they met, where they had their first kiss, his old apartment, her old apartment, the theater where they had their first date, and places where they had fought.

One woman returned to her small Midwestern town to try to recall what she had ever seen in her husband. She explained,

> Part of me wondered if I had just been a naive schoolgirl. I wondered if maybe I had fallen for this guy because he was older than the boys who usually paid attention to me. Maybe I was just flattered. Maybe I married him because my parents didn't approve. I spent more than an hour one afternoon sitting in my car outside the building where he used to work. There was a time I used to park in that same spot and wait for him to get off work. Boy, did that bring back memories. And you know what? I remembered how I used to feel about him and why. I think what I learned was that I really did love him, at least at one time. Of course, that did not mean that I could not fall out of love. But it was important to get a good understanding of what my feelings were so that I could understand what they had become.

These and other examples lead me to suggest that counselors and therapists might consider some form of "place therapy" when working with their clients. Therapists often use an assortment of procedures to help clients get in touch with their feelings, including feelings about events from years earlier. My work tells me that one way to reach some of these emotions is to surround the person with visual and other sensory cues associated with relevant memories. Most of the participants we placed in the unfinished-business category had already reached this insight. They were seeing a psychological counselor at the time they made their trip. This is not to say that visiting a place from the past will necessarily be therapeutic. But these kinds of trips, under the guidance of a professional counselor, might provide therapists with one more tool they can use to help their clients.

Residential Mobility

Moving into a new home is rarely easy. There are the obvious adventures associated with finding a new place to live, packing, traveling, physically transporting belongings, unpacking, and constructing a new living space. But moving can also mean finding a new doctor, meeting new neighbors, attending a new school, working with new colleagues, starting new habits, and missing old friends. The entire experience can be exciting, sad, frightening, and exhausting.

As described in the last chapter, the frequency with which people put themselves through this experience has implications for their psychological and physical health. But changing addresses may also have consequences far beyond personal challenges and difficulties. A relatively new but growing field of study suggests that how often we move can affect the way we think of ourselves, the nature of our communities, and even the kind of culture we live in.

Rootlessness and Independent Selves

I have argued throughout this book that we often incorporate significant places from our past into our sense of self. If that is the case, then it is not difficult to imagine that people who moved frequently from place to place during childhood will have very different self-concepts from people who moved rarely or not at all.

Psychologists sometimes look at self-concept in terms of interdependence and independence.[2] People with an interdependent self-concept tend to think of themselves in terms of their relationships with their family and their community. People with an independent self-concept are more likely to define themselves in terms of their individual characteristics. When asked to describe herself, a woman with an interdependent self-concept is likely to include her family, the social organizations she belongs to, and her place in the community. A woman with an independent self-concept is less likely to mention any of these things. Instead she may focus on her skills, personal achievements, and personality traits when describing who she is. One woman sees herself as a part of the community; the other thinks of herself as an individual.

Psychologist Shigehiro Oishi has argued that people who change residences frequently are more likely to develop an independent self-concept than those who live in one place for an extended period.[3] For example, a person is unlikely to develop an identity as a New Yorker, a Southerner, or a suburbanite if he or she has lived in such places for only a short time. Similarly, if your life consists of a series of different friends, different neighbors, and different employers that change every few years, you probably won't describe yourself in terms of your relationship with any of these groups. Instead, Oishi maintains, people who move frequently come to define themselves in terms of the attributes they carry with them from place to place.

Whether we think of ourselves in terms of the community we belong to or as individuals has many important psychological implications. Chief among these is what makes us happy.[4] People who tie their identities to others are happy when they feel they belong to, and are supported by, their families and communities. People who think of themselves in individualistic terms are happy to the extent that they like the kind of person they believe themselves to be. The former don't need personal achievements to feel good about themselves, whereas the latter can be happy without fitting into a larger organization.

Mobile and Stable Communities

Like individuals, neighborhoods, communities, and towns also differ in terms of residential mobility. Some neighborhoods, like many in Las Vegas, Nevada, experience a constant flow of people coming and going. In contrast, residents in communities like Jonestown, Pennsylvania, see relatively few moving vans in front of their neighbors' homes. Given a choice, most people prefer the more stable community. Knowing your neighbors and watching their children grow up is part of many people's image of the ideal lifestyle. Realtors are well aware of these preferences and often woo potential home buyers by pointing to the stability of a neighborhood.

Not surprisingly, the level of connection people feel with their community is tied to how long they have lived there. After living in Charleston or Omaha for many years, residents come to think of themselves as a part of their city. In larger metropolitan areas, citizens might identify with the section of the city they live in, such as Harlem or Nob Hill. Over time, people start to care about the quality of the parks and the schools, the issues that face elected officials, and the future direction of their community. In short, they begin to form roots. But this sense of belonging takes time to develop, probably many years. People who stay in one place for only a year or two are unlikely to think of themselves in terms of where they live. And cities with a high percentage of individuals who feel no particular tie to the community are different in important ways from cities where most residents feel they belong.

One team of researchers demonstrated the difference between stable and mobile communities by looking at attendance figures for major-league baseball games.[5] Although people attend games for many reasons, the investigators identified two primary motives. Some people go to baseball games because of a long-standing association with the team. They see the team as a part of their community, and they want to support the players. Other people attend games for the entertainment value. More specifically, these individuals like to cheer for successful teams and enjoy watching when "their" team wins.

As a rule, attendance at sporting events goes up during winning seasons and down during losing seasons. But is this tendency to support winners and shun losers the same for every team? Remember some fans attend games because the team is part of a community they identify with, not because the team is winning or losing. We would expect to find more of these team-focused fans in a residentially stable community than in a mobile one. Thus, the degree to which attendance patterns reflect the team's place in the standings might vary from location to location, depending on the city's average amount of residential mobility.

To test this possibility, the researchers first examined census data to determine the level of residential mobility in each American city with a major-league team. They discovered substantial differences among cities. Two out of every three residents in Pittsburgh (home of the Pirates) have lived in their present home for at least five years. However, this is true for only 42 percent of the people who live in Phoenix (home of the Diamondbacks). The investigators then looked at how much attendance fluctuated in each city depending on its team's win-loss record. They found that in residentially stable cities like Pittsburgh, New York, and Philadelphia, people tended to buy tickets with relatively little concern for how the team was performing on the field. In contrast, fans in cities with highly mobile populations, like Phoenix, Atlanta, and Denver, were more likely to belong to the fair-weather variety. These individuals like to watch when the team is doing well but have no particular reason to support the home team when the product on the field is not very entertaining. Researchers also have found this pattern when comparing baseball attendance figures for residentially mobile and stable cities in Japan.[6]

Residentially stable communities have a number of advantages over communities with mobile populations. In general, people who identify with their community make better citizens. The longer people live in the same place, the more likely they are to vote.[7] Communities with residents who stay in one place also have lower crime rates.[8] These stable residents are also more likely to support local interests, even if doing so takes more money out of their pockets. One study looked at the percentage of Minnesota residents who purchased "critical habitat" license plates.[9] The proceeds from these plates went to preserving natural wildlife habitats in the state. Sales were considerably higher in the areas with a large number of residentially stable citizens. Apparently, residents who had lived in their homes for a lengthy period cared enough about their local community to pay the additional $30 for the special license plate. All of these findings hold up even after researchers account for other possible causes, like income, age, education, and political affiliation. In other words, all else being equal, the length of time the average resident has lived in one place tells us a lot about what kind of place it is.

Mobility and Culture

In 1831, Alexis de Tocqueville, a twenty-five-year-old sent to the United States by the French government to study American prisons, set out on an extensive tour of this relatively young nation. Tocqueville described his observations of the American people and the unique features of their nascent culture in two books that made him famous and have been widely cited ever since. Among the many differences Tocqueville saw between Americans and Europeans was America's "instability of character."[10] The typical American, Tocqueville wrote, "takes up, quits and takes up again ten trades in his lifetime; he changes his residence ceaselessly and continually forms new enterprises. . . . [He] will carefully construct a home in which to spend his old age and sell it before the roof is on."

Much has changed in the nearly two centuries since Tocqueville made his observations. But remnants survive of the American propensity to sell the house before the roof is on. Americans change addresses far more frequently than citizens in most other developed countries.[11] We move about twice as often as people in England, Germany, Sweden, Japan, France, the Netherlands, Belgium, or Ireland. Only residents in New Zealand, Australia, and Canada can keep up with our pace.

At a professional conference a few years ago, I found myself talking with a German psychologist who had made frequent visits to America. When I asked him about the differences he saw between the two countries, he answered without hesitation. He was amazed at how frequently his American colleagues moved. This psychologist typically visited the United States every two or three years, and it seemed to him that each time he visited his American friends, they were living in a new house. This experience contrasted sharply with his own. Not only had he resided in a single house his entire life, but it was the same house in which his parents, grandparents, and great grandparents had lived.

If communities with frequent movers are different from those made up of relatively stable residents, what differences might we find between residentially mobile and residentially stable countries? Some psychologists have argued that this tendency to change homes not only is a feature of, but has also shaped, American culture.

Cross-cultural researchers often place cultures along an individualistic-collectivist continuum.[12] At one end we find cultures that emphasize the uniqueness of the individual. Children raised in these cultures are taught to identify the special talents and characteristics that make them different from everyone else. People living in individualistic cultures tend to have independent self-concepts. They want to stand out. They want to be the best. In contrast, people living in collectivist cultures are more interested in being part of a larger group, such as a family, community, or nation. They tend to have interdependent self-concepts. Children growing up in collectivist cultures learn to avoid drawing attention to themselves. They prefer to fit in, to find their place in the larger group.

Studies find that Americans are among the most individualistic people in the world.[13] Perhaps not coincidentally, Americans are also among the most residentially mobile. Many centuries ago in Europe, residential mobility was rare. People were born into, and lived their lives within, a social network made up of others in the same community. Identities were based on where one lived and the social network one lived in.[14] When people thought about who they were, they focused on the relatively permanent and stable groups to which they belonged. Names also reflected this connection between person and place. I often find it amusing when people refer to the painter of the *Mona Lisa* as "da Vinci." Da Vinci was not Leonardo's last name, popular novels and movies notwithstanding. Rather, the man's name was Leonardo. The "da Vinci" part tells us about his hometown. He was from Vinci.

The connection between place and person is far more tenuous in today's mobile society. As a result of the constant movement Tocqueville described,

Americans and others who live in mobile cultures tend to define themselves in terms of the personal characteristics they carry with them wherever they go. Whereas medieval Europeans based their self-concepts on who their parents were and what town they lived in, Americans are more likely to think of themselves in terms of their skills, achievements, and personality traits.

If cultural differences can be traced in part to residential mobility, another interesting possibility emerges. In recent years, we have seen an increase in residential relocation in many parts of the world.[15] Modernization often translates into an increase in residential mobility. People who a generation ago might have lived their entire lives in one community now pursue career and life opportunities in different cities and, increasingly, in different countries. Whether these changes will result in significant cultural shifts remains to be seen. However, studies find that the longer immigrants from collectivist cultures live in individualistic cultures, the more individualistic they become. One team of Canadian investigators found that it took about three generations for immigrants from collectivist Asian countries to develop self-concepts that resembled those of the typical individualistic Canadian.[16] Of course, residential mobility is but one source driving some of these cultural changes. But it may turn out to be one of the most powerful.

Independent Living

Although each life unfolds in its own unique way, most cultures have a template for how the typical life is suppose to progress. In our culture, children stay with their parents through adolescence. Then they move away from home, develop careers, find life partners, establish their own homes, and have their own children who stay with them through adolescence. Adults enjoy the roles of grandparent and maybe great-grandparent. They retire and eventually move into a facility designed for someone their age or with their health issues.

In addition to the many, many exceptions to this scenario, the problem with this template is that nobody seems to have asked senior citizens what they want. As it turns out, the vast majority of people in their retirement years do not want to move out of their homes.[17] And, for the most part, they don't. In 2008, only 4 percent of Americans sixty-five and older were living in a nursing or assisted-living facility.[18] Today, numerous government and private organizations have been created to help older Americans maintain "independent-living" situations in their own homes. By providing assistance with transportation and various daily chores, these agencies allow elderly citizens to live under their own roofs for as long as possible.

But why do the vast majority of elderly Americans prefer to stay in their own homes? Why not move into a place with fewer challenges and a staff that will attend to many of their daily needs? Psychologists have identified several reasons for this preference, but each explanation is a variation on the observation that elderly adults, like people of all ages, feel a psychological connection with their homes.

As a rule, people move less frequently as they get older.[19] When they approach middle age, people tend to settle into one home where they raise their children and become part of the community. Moving to satisfy career opportunities becomes less of a concern, and it is not uncommon for people approaching retirement age to have lived in the same place for twenty or thirty years. This stability generatess countless memories associated with a particular home. In addition, older adults typically spend more of their day inside than do younger adults.[20] As a result, elderly citizens' self-concepts may be even more closely tied to where they live than is the case for younger adults.

The objects inside older people's homes may also be linked to their personal identities.[21] Homes of retired adults are often filled with personally meaningful photographs. Gifts from special people, souvenirs from special places, and mementos from special times are also common. Places and furnishings in the home can be associated with significant people and events. There may be curtains picked out with a deceased sister, a kitchen table where the family used to gather, or a backyard garden where a spouse grew vegetables every summer. Removing people from these objects and places can be tantamount to severing an important part of their self-concept. For these reasons, when moving to a new home becomes necessary, the more personal objects that can be taken to the new residence, the better.[22]

Staying in one's own home also provides a sense of personal control. Just as eight-year-olds build tree houses and private forts as a way to establish a sense of mastery over their expanding worlds, eighty-year-olds can rearrange furniture and decorate their living space as a way to exercise control over their shrinking ones. I spoke with a woman recently who works with a government agency in Sacramento, helping elderly citizens stay in their homes. She explained that it was not enough for these individuals simply to reside in the same house they had known for many years. Rather, it was important that they retained a sense of control over what happened in that home, even if they physically could not do much of the actual work. In particular, she thought it was critical for aides and health-care workers not to enter the front door of the home until they are asked. As described in chapter 2, in our society visitors are not allowed to enter another person's home without permission. We knock on the door or ring the bell and wait until we are invited in. When control over who enters the home is relinquished, the older adult's sense that this is his or her own place of residence may be lost.

Researchers find a connection between elderly adults' losing a sense of personal control and many psychological and physical health problems.[23] Although we often experience a desire to do things for our older relatives, studies suggest that this may be the exact opposite of what they need. In one classic experiment, a team of researchers altered the way staff members treated one floor of a retirement facility.[24] Instead of emphasizing how much the staff could do for them, they encouraged residents to rearrange their furniture (with assistance), construct their own daily-activity schedule, and even to select and take care of their own plants. A comparable floor in the same facility was treated in the same we'll-do-it-for-you style as always. Within weeks, differences between the two groups were evident. Residents encouraged to take charge of their lives were more active and happier than the other group. Most important, when the researchers returned to the facility eighteen months later, they found that 30 percent of the residents on the traditional floor had passed away in the interim. This contrasted with a 15 percent mortality rate for the residents who were encouraged to stay in control of their worlds.[25]

And so there we have it. The connection many people feel with their homes begins in childhood and continues throughout the life cycle. The places we live in become part of who we are. They provide landscapes for our lives and receptacles for our memories. Yet, our memories and the bonds we feel with our homes are always under siege by the passage of time. Fortunately, as many people have discovered, the connection can be strengthened with a little visit.

Notes

Chapter 1

1. "2004 American Community Survey," U.S. Census Bureau, accessed September 21, 2010, http://factfinder.census.gov/servlet/ADPTable?_bm=y&-geo_id=01000US&-qr_name=ACS_2004_EST_G00_DP4&-ds_name=ACS_2004_EST_G00_&-_lang=en&-_caller=geoselect&-state=adp&-format=http://factfinder.census.gov.

2. Sam Roberts, "Census Finds Most Americans on the Move: Fewer Than 1 in 10 Households Has Kept Same Home Since 1959," *San Jose Mercury News*, December 13, 1994, 12A.

3. U.S. Census Bureau, (2004) "American Community Survey."

4. "Three Hollywood Stars Showed Up at Wichita Couple's Doorstep," *San Jose Mercury News*, December 9, 2001, 2A.

Chapter 2

1. Lawrence J. Roderick, "What Makes a House a Home?" *Environment and Behavior* 19, no. 2 (March 1987): 154–68; Donna Birdwell-Pheasant and Denise Lawrence-Zuniga, "Introduction: Houses and Families in Europe," in *House Life: Space, Place and Family in Europe*, ed. Donna Birdwell-Pheasant and Denise Lawrence-Zuniga (Oxford, UK: Berg, 1999), 1–16.

2. Robert Frost, "The Death of the Hired Man," *Pocket Anthology of Robert Frost's Poems* (New York: Pocket Books, 1977), 165.

3. Jude Cassidy and Phillip R. Shaver, eds., *Handbook of Attachment: Theory, Research, and Clinical Applications* (New York: Guilford, 1999).

4. David G. Myers, *The Pursuit of Happiness: Who Is Happy, and Why* (New York: Morrow, 1992).

5. Harold M. Proshansky, Abbe K. Fabian, and Robert Kaminoff, "Place-Identity: Physical World Socialization and the Self," *Journal of Environmental Psychology* 3, no. 1 (March 1983): 57–83.

6. David M. Buss, "Evolutionary Personality Psychology," *Annual Review of Psychology* 42 (1991): 459–91.

7. Roy F. Baumeister and Mark R. Leary, "The Need to Belong: Desire for Interpersonal Attachments As a Fundamental Human Motivation," *Psychological Bulletin* 117, no. 3 (May 1995): 497–529.

8. Roger A. Powell, "Animal Home Ranges and Territories and Home Range Estimations," in *Research Techniques in Animal Ecology*, ed. Luigi Boitani and Todd K. Fuller (New York: Columbia University Press, 2000), 65–110.

9. Douglas H. MacDonald and Barry S. Hewlett, "Reproductive Interests and Forager Mobility," *Current Anthropology* 40, no. 4 (August–October 1999): 501–23.

10. William Van Vliet, "Exploring the Fourth Environment: An Examination of the Home Range of City and Suburban Teenagers," *Environment and Behavior* 15, no. 5 (September 1983): 567–88; Paul Webley, "Sex Differences in Home Range and Cognitive Maps in Eight-Year Old Children," *Journal of Environmental Psychology* 1, no. 4 (December 1981): 293–302.

11. Christine R. Maher and Dale F. Lott, "Definitions of Territoriality Used in the Study of Variation in Vertebrate Spacing Systems," *Animal Behaviour* 49, no. 6 (June 1995): 1581–97.

12. Barbara B. Brown, "Territoriality," in *Handbook of Environmental Psychology*, ed. Daniel Stokels and Irwin Altman (New York: Wiley, 1987), 505–31.

13. Kenji Omata, "Territoriality in the House and Its Relationship to the Use of Rooms and the Psychological Well-Being of Japanese Married Women," *Journal of Environmental Psychology* 15, no. 2 (June 1995): 147–54.

14. Neil Wollman, Benita M. Kelly, and Kenneth S. Bordens, "Environmental and Intrapersonal Predictors of Reactions to Potential Territorial Intrusions in the Workplace," *Environment and Behavior* 26, no. 2 (March 1994): 179–94.

15. R. Barry Ruback and Daniel Juieng, "Territorial Defense in Parking Lots: Retaliation against Waiting Drivers," *Journal of Applied Social Psychology* 27, no. 9 (May 1997): 821–34.

16. Isabel Fonseca, *Bury Me Standing: The Gypsies and Their Journey* (New York: Vintage, 1995).

17. Fonseca, *Bury Me Standing.*

18. Carol M. Werner, Irwin Altman, and Diana Oxley, "Temporal Aspects of Homes: A Transactional Perspective," in *Home Environments*, ed. Irwin Altman and Carol M. Werner (New York: Plenum, 1985), 1–32.

19. Gordon H. Bower, "Mood and Memory," *American Psychologist* 36, no. 2 (February 1981): 129–48.

20. Daniel T. Gilbert, Erin Driver-Linn, and Timothy D. Wilson, "The Trouble with Vronsky: Impact Bias in the Forecasting of Future Affective States," in *The Wisdom of Feeling: Psychological Processes in Emotional Intelligence*, ed. Lisa Feldman Barrett and Peter Salovey (New York: Guilford, 2002), 114–43.

21. Terence R. Mitchell et al., "Temporal Adjustments in the Evaluation of Events: The 'Rosy View,'" *Journal of Experimental Social Psychology* 33, no. 4 (July 1997): 421–48.

22. William Damon and Daniel Hart, "The Development of Self-understanding from Infancy through Adolescence," *Child Development* 53, no. 4 (August 1982): 841–64.

23. Deborah Kendzierski, "Exercise Self-schemata: Cognitive and Behavioral Correlates," *Health Psychology* 9, no. 1 (January 1990): 69–82.

24. William James, *Psychology: Briefer Course* (1892; New York: Collier Books, 1962), 190.

25. Stefan E. Hormuth, *The Ecology of the Self: Relocation and Self-concept Change* (Cambridge: Cambridge University Press, 1990).

26. Marlene Mackie, "The Domestication of Self: Gender Comparisons of Self-imagery and Self-esteem," *Social Psychology Quarterly* 46, no. 4 (December 1983): 343–50.

27. Stephanie M. Clancy and Stephen J. Dollinger, "Photographic Depictions of the Self: Gender and Age Differences in Social Connectedness," *Sex Roles* 29, nos. 7–8 (October 1993): 477–95.

28. Arthur Aron, "Self and Close Relationships," in *Handbook of Self and Identity*, ed. Mark R. Leary and June P. Tangney (New York: Guilford, 2003), 442–61.

29. Colin M. MacLeod, "Half a Century of Research on the Stroop Effect: An Integrative Review," *Psychological Bulletin* 109, no. 2 (March 1991): 163–203.

30. Arthur Aron et al., "Close Relationships As Including Other in the Self," *Journal of Personality and Social Psychology* 60, no. 2 (February 1991): 241–53.

31. Michael A. Hogg, "Self-categorization and Subjective Uncertainty Resolution: Cognitive and Motivational Facets of Social Identity and Group Membership," in *The Social Mind: Cognitive and Motivational Aspects of Interpersonal Behavior*, ed. Joseph P. Forgas, Kipling D. Williams, and Ladd Wheeler (Cambridge: Cambridge University Press, 2001), 323–49.

32. Manford H. Kuhn and Thomas S. McPartland, "An Empirical Investigation of Self Attitudes," *American Sociological Review* 19, no. 1 (February 1954): 68–76.

33. Eliot R. Smith, Susan Coats, and Dustin Walling, "Overlapping Mental Representations of Self, In-Group, and Partner: Further Response Time Evidence and a Connectionist Model," *Personality and Social Psychology Bulletin* 25, no. 7 (July 1999): 873–82.

34. Anthony G. Greenwald, Jacqueline E. Pickrell, and Shelly D. Farnham, "Implicit Partisanship: Taking Sides for No Reason," *Journal of Personality and Social Psychology* 83, no. 2 (August 2002): 367–79.

35. Hogg, "Self-categorization."

36. Russell W. Belk, "Possessions and the Extended Self," *Journal of Consumer Research* 15, no. 2 (September 1988): 139–68.

37. Beverly MacLeod, "In the Wake of Disaster," *Psychology Today* 18, no. 10 (October 1984): 54–57.

38. James K. Beggan, "On the Social Nature of Nonsocial Perception: The Mere Ownership Effect," *Journal of Personality and Social Psychology* 62, no. 2 (February 1992): 229–37.

39. Jozef M. Nuttin, "Affective Consequences of Mere Ownership: The Name Letter Effect in Twelve European Languages," *European Journal of Social Psychology* 17, no. 4 (October–December 1987): 381–402.

40. Brett W. Pelham, Matthew C. Mirenberg, and John T. Jones, "Why Susie Sells Seashells by the Seashore: Implicit Egotism and Major Life Decisions," *Journal of Personality and Social Psychology* 82, no. 4 (April 2002): 469–87; Brett W. Pelham et al., "Assessing the Validity of Implicit Egotism: A Reply to Gallucci (2003)," *Journal of Personality and Social Psychology* 85, no. 5 (November 2003): 800–807.

41. John T. Jones et al., "How Do I Love Thee? Let Me Count the Js: Implicit Egotism and Interpersonal Attraction," *Journal of Personality and Social Psychology* 87, no. 5 (November 2004): 665–83.

42. Proshansky, Fabian, and Kaminoff, "Place Identity"; Clare Cooper Marcus, *House As a Mirror of Self: Exploring the Deeper Meaning of Home* (Berkeley, CA: Conari Press, 1995); Irwin Altman and Carol M. Werner, eds., *Home Environments* (New York: Plenum, 1985).

43. Russell W. Belk, "Identity and the Relevance of Market, Personal, and Community Objects," in *Marketing and Semiotics: New Directions in the Study of Signs for Sale*, ed. Jean Umiker-Sebeok (Berlin: Mouton de Gruyter, 1987), 151–64.

44. James, *Psychology*, 191.

45. Julia Omarzu, "A Disclosure Decision Model: Determining How and When Individuals Will Self-disclose," *Personality and Social Psychology Review* 4, no. 2 (April 2000): 174–85.

46. Barbara B. Brown and Douglas D. Perkins, "Disruptions in Place Attachment," in *Place Attachment: Human Behavior and Environment*, ed. Irwin Altman and Setha M. Low (New York: Plenum, 1992), 279–304.

47. Belk, "Possessions."

48. Perla Korosec-Serfaty, "Experience and Use of the Dwelling," in *Home Environments*, ed. Irwin Altman and Carol M. Werner (New York: Plenum, 1985), 65–86.

49. Roy F. Baumeister, *Identity: Cultural Change and the Struggle for Self* (New York: Oxford University Press, 1986).

50. Jake Halpern, *Braving Home: Dispatches from the Underwater Town, the Lava-Side Inn, and Other Extreme Locations* (Boston: Houghton-Mifflin, 2003).

51. Halpern, *Braving Home*, 47.

52. Mary Comerio, *Disaster Hits Home: New Policy for Urban Housing Recovery* (Berkeley: University of California Press, 1998).

53. Brad Heath, Paul Overberg, and Haya El Nasser, "Census Shows Katrina's Effects on Populations," *USA Today*, March 27, 2007, 7A; Campbell Robertson, "Suspense Builds over Census for New Orleans," *New York Times*, April 7, 2010, A19(L).

54. Jerry M. Burger, "Solitude," in *Encyclopedia of Mental Health*, ed. Howard S. Friedman (San Diego, CA: Academic Press, 1998), 563–69.

55. "Administration for Children and Families," U.S. Department of Health and Human Services, www.acf.dhhs.gov/programs/cb/publications/cm02/summary.htm.

56. Kristen C. Kling et al., "Exploring the Influence of Personality on Depressive Symptoms and Self-esteem across a Significant Life Transition," *Journal of Personality and Social Psychology* 85, no. 5 (November 2003): 922–32.

Chapter 3

1. Harlene Hayne, "Infant Memory Development: Implications for Childhood Amnesia," *Developmental Review* 24, no. 1 (March 2004): 33–73.

2. Mark L. Howe and Mary L. Courage, "The Emergence and Early Development of Autobiographical Memory," *Psychological Review* 104, no. 3 (July 1997): 400–533.

3. Larry Felson et al., "Variability in Early Communicative Development," *Monographs of the Society for Research in Child Development* 59, no. 5, serial no. 242 (1994).

4. Robyn Fiviush, Jacquelyn T. Gray, and Fayne A. Fromhoff, "Two-Year-Olds Talk about the Past," *Cognitive Development* 2, no. 4 (October 1987): 393–409.

5. Edith Cobb, *The Ecology of Imagination in Childhood* (New York: Columbia University Press, 1977).

6. Edith Cobb, "The Ecology of Imagination in Childhood," *Daedalus* 88, no. 3 (Summer 1959): 537–48.

7. Jerry M. Burger, *The Desire for Control: Personality, Social and Clinical Perspectives* (New York: Plenum Press, 1992).

8. Roger A. Hart, *Children's Experience of Place* (New York: Irvington Publishers, 1979).

9. David Sobel, *Mapmaking with Children: Sense of Place Education for the Elementary School Years* (Portsmouth, NH: Heinemann, 1998).

10. Julie Sevrens Lyons, "An Alarm over Kids' Weight—Tipping the Scales: Growing Numbers of America's Children Are Overweight," *San Jose Mercury News*, March 7, 2004, 1A.

11. David Sobel, *Children's Special Places: Exploring the Role of Forts, Dens, and Bush Houses in Middle Childhood* (Tucson, AZ: Zephyr Press, 1993).

12. Sobel, *Children's Special Places*, 25–26.

13. Clare Cooper Marcus, "Remembrance of Landscapes Past," *Landscape* 22, no. 3 (June 1978): 35–43.

14. Kalevi Mikael Korpela, "Place-Identity As a Product of Environmental Self-regulation," in *Giving Places Meaning*, ed. Linda Groat (London: Academic Press, 1995), 115–30.

15. David Sobel, "A Place in the World: Adults' Memories of Childhood Special Places," *Children's Environments Quarterly* 7, no. 4 (December 1990): 5–12.

16. Sarah K. Zeegers, Christine A. Readdick, and Salley Hansen-Gandy, "Daycare Children's Establishment of Territory to Experience Privacy," *Children's Environments* 11, no. 4 (December 1994): 265–71.

Chapter 4

1. "'Dallas' Is First, Napa Third," *San Francisco Examiner*, February 24, 1982, E17.

2. *Johnny Goes Home*, written by Johnny Carson, produced by David Lowe Jr. (Carson Productions, 1982).

3. William Saroyan, *Places Where I've Done Time* (New York: Delta, 1972), 110–11.

4. Loren Eiseley, *The Night Country* (New York: Charles Scribner's Sons, 1971), 233–34.

5. Personal e-mail communication with Michael Chabon, July 14, 1995.

6. Interview with William Styron by Bob Edwards, "William Styron Publishes First Fiction Work in 15 Years," *Morning Edition*, segment #14, National Public Radio, February 1, 1994.

7. Eric Lax, *Woody Allen: A Biography* (New York: Knopf, 1991).

8. Lax, *Woody Allen*, 20.

9. Ben Brantley, "The World That Created August Wilson," *New York Times*, February 5, 1995, H1.

10. Michalene Busico, "Bringing It All Back Home: Ernest Gaines Is a Southern Writer with a Northern California Address," *San Jose Mercury News*, January 16, 1994, AB15.

11. Busico, "Bringing It All Back Home," AB3.

12. Julia Omarzu, "A Disclosure Decision Model: Determining How and When Individuals Will Self-disclose," *Personality and Social Psychology Review* 4, no. 2 (April 2000): 174–85.

13. John H. Harvey and Julia Omarzu, "Minding the Close Relationship," *Personality and Social Psychology Review* 1, no. 3 (July 1997): 224–40.

14. Kathryn Dindia and Mike Allen, "Sex Differences in Self-disclosure: A Meta-analysis," *Psychological Bulletin* 112, no. 1 (July 1992): 106–24.

15. Jerry M. Burger, "Solitude," in *Encyclopedia of Mental Health*, ed. Howard S. Friedman (San Diego, CA: Academic Press, 1998), 563–69.

16. Eiseley, *Night Country*, 232–33.

17. Daniel T. Gilbert, Erin Driver-Linn, and Timothy D. Wilson, "The Trouble with Vronsky: Impact Bias in the Forecasting of Future Affective States," in *The*

Wisdom of Feeling: Psychological Processes in Emotional Intelligence, ed. Lisa Feldman Barrett and Peter Salovey (New York: Guilford, 2002), 114–43.

Chapter 5

1. Jefferson A. Singer, "Special Issue: Narrative Identity and Meaning Making across the Adult Lifespan," *Journal of Personality* 72, no. 3 (June 2004): 437–657.

2. Anne E. Wilson and Michael Ross, "The Frequency of Temporal-Self and Social Comparisons in People's Personal Appraisals," *Journal of Personality and Social Psychology* 78, no. 5 (May 2000): 928–42.

3. Erich Fromm, *Escape from Freedom* (New York: Avon, 1965).

4. Erik H. Erikson, *Identity: Youth and Crisis* (New York: Norton, 1968).

5. "New Move for Old Home of Jimi Hendrix's," *San Jose Mercury News*, September 12, 2005, 7A.

6. "Beatle Abode Set for Destruction," *San Jose Mercury News*, September 10, 2005, 2A.

7. Richard Sandomir, "A Fight to Save the House That Built Ruth: School in Baltimore Says It Has a History Worth Preserving," *New York Times*, April 18, 2010, S1–S2.

8. Jerry Adler et al., "In Search of the Spiritual," *Newsweek*, September 2, 2005, 56–62.

9. Adler et al., "In Search of the Spiritual."

Chapter 6

1. Interview with Andrew Jarecki by Terry Gross, "Filmmaker Andrew Jarecki," *Fresh Air from WHYY*, National Public Radio, June 24, 2003.

2. Interview with Jarecki, "Filmmaker."

3. Interview with Jarecki, "Filmmaker."

4. Bridget F. Grant, "Estimates of U.S. Children Exposed to Alcohol Abuse and Dependence in the Family," *American Journal of Public Health* 90, no. 1 (January 2000): 112–15.

5. Grant, "Estimates."

6. U.S. Department of Health and Human Services, *Child Maltreatment 2003* (Washington, DC: Government Printing Office, 2005).

7. "Long-Term Consequences of Child Abuse and Neglect," National Clearinghouse on Child Abuse and Neglect Information, U.S. Department of Health and Human Services, accessed July 2005, http://nccanch.acf.hhs.gov.

8. Amy B. Silverman, Helen Z. Reinherz, and Rose M. Giaconia, "The Long-Term Sequelae of Child and Adolescent Abuse: A Longitudinal Community Study," *Child Abuse and Neglect* 20, no. 8 (August 1996): 709–23.

9. Karen S. Peterson, "Bullies Shove Their Way into the Nation's Schools," *USA Today*, September 7, 1999, D1.

10. "Facts for Families: Bullying," American Academy of Child and Adolescent Psychiatry, accessed May 2008, www.aacap.org/cs/root/facts_for_families/bullying.

11. Robin M. Kowalski, *Complaining, Teasing, and Other Annoying Behaviors* (New Haven, CT: Yale University Press, 2003).

12. Peter Schworm, "State Bill Targeting Bullying Approved: Aims at Schools, Cyber Behavior: One of Toughest Measures in U.S.," *Boston Globe*, April 30, 2010, A1.

13. Ronnie Janoff-Bulman, *Shattered Assumptions: Toward a New Psychology of Trauma* (New York: Free Press, 1992).

14. James W. Pennebaker, "Confession, Inhibition, and Disease," in *Advances in Experimental Social Psychology*, ed. Leonard Berkowitz (New York: Academic Press, 1989), 211–44.

15. Joanne Frattaroli, "Experimental Disclosure and Its Moderators: A Meta-analysis," *Psychological Bulletin* 132, no. 6 (November 2006): 823–65; Laura A. King and K. N. Miner, "Writing about Perceived Benefits of Traumatic Events: Implications for Physical Health," *Personality and Social Psychology Bulletin* 26, no. 2 (February 2000): 220–30.

16. Jerry Suls and Barbara Fletcher, "The Relative Efficacy of Avoidant and Nonavoidant Coping Strategies: A Meta-analysis," *Health Psychology* 4, no. 3 (May 1985): 249–88.

17. Camille B. Wortman and Roxane Cohen Silver, "The Myths of Coping with Loss Revisited," in *Handbook of Bereavement Research: Consequences, Coping, and Care*, ed. Margaret S. Stroebe et al. (Washington, DC: American Psychological Association, 2001), 405–29.

18. Kevin Ann Oltjenbruns, "Developmental Context of Childhood: Grief and Regrief Phenomena," in *Handbook of Bereavement Research: Consequences, Coping, and Care*, ed. Margaret S. Stroebe et al. (Washington, DC: American Psychological Association, 2001), 169–97.

19. Oltjenbruns, "Developmental Context."

Chapter 7

1. Mary Edwards Wertsch, *Military Brats: Legacies of Childhood inside the Fortress* (New York: Harmony Books, 1991).

2. Scott M. Myers, "Residential Mobility As a Way of Life: Evidence of Intergenerational Similarities," *Journal of Marriage and the Family* 61, no. 4 (November 1999): 871–80.

3. David Wood et al., "Impact of Family Relocation on Children's Growth, Development, School Function, and Behavior," *Journal of the American Medical Association* 270, no. 11 (September 15, 1993): 1334–38.

4. T. Jellyman and N. Spencer, "Residential Mobility in Childhood and Health Outcomes: A Systematic Review," *Journal of Epidemiology and Community Health* 62, no. 7 (July 2008): 584–92; Maxia Dong et al., "Childhood Residential Mobility and Multiple Health Risks during Adolescence and Adulthood," *Archives of Pediatrics and Adolescent Medicine* 159, no. 12 (December 2005): 1104–10.

5. Emma K. Adams and Lindsay Chase-Lansdale, "Home Sweet Home(s): Parental Separations, Residential Moves, and Adjustment Problems in Low-Income Adolescent Girls," *Developmental Psychology* 38, no. 5 (September 2000): 792–805.

6. Emma K. Adams, "Beyond Quality: Parental and Residential Stability and Children's Adjustment," *Current Directions in Psychological Science* 13, no. 3 (October 2004): 210–13.

7. Shigehiro Oishi, "The Psychology of Residential Mobility: Implications for the Self, Social Relationships, and Well-Being," *Perspectives on Psychological Science* 5, no. 1 (January 2010): 5–21.

8. Wood et al., "Impact of Family Relocation."

9. David G. Myers, *The Pursuit of Happiness: Who Is Happy, and Why* (New York: Morrow, 1992).

10. Shigehiro Oishi and Ulrich Schimmack, "Residential Mobility, Well-Being and Mortality," *Journal of Personality and Social Psychology* 98, no. 6 (2010): 980–94.

Chapter 8

1. *Reschool Yourself*, www.reschoolyourself.com.

2. Susan E. Cross and Laura Madson, "Models of the Self: Self-construals and Gender," *Psychological Bulletin* 122, no. 1 (July 1997): 5–37.

3. Shigehiro Oishi, "The Psychology of Residential Mobility: Implications for the Self, Social Relationships, and Well-Being," *Perspectives on Psychological Science* 5, no. 1 (January 2010): 5–21.

4. Hazel R. Markus and Shinobu Kitayama, "Culture and the Self: Implications for Cognition, Emotion, and Motivation," *Psychological Review* 98, no. 2 (April 1991): 224–53.

5. Shigehiro Oishi et al., "The Socioecological Model of Procommunity Action: The Benefits of Residential Stability," *Journal of Personality and Social Psychology* 93, no. 5 (November 2007): 831–44.

6. Shigehiro Oishi, Keiko Ishii, and Janetta Lun, "Residential Mobility and Conditionality of Group Identification," *Journal of Experimental Social Psychology* 45, no. 4 (July 2009): 913–19.

7. Benjamin Highton, "Residential Mobility, Community Mobility, and Electoral Participation," *Political Behavior* 22, no. 2 (June 2000): 109–20.

8. Robert J. Sampson, Stephen W. Raudenbush, and Felton Earls, "Neighborhoods and Violent Crime: A Multilevel Study of Evidence," *Science* 277, no. 5328 (August 15, 1997): 918–27.

9. Oishi et al., "Socioecological Model."

10. Alexis de Tocqueville, *Democracy in America* (1835; New York: Norton, 2007), 622.

11. Larry Long, "Changing Residence: Comparative Perspectives on Its Relationship to Age, Sex, and Marital Status," *Populations Studies* 46, no. 1 (March 1992): 141–58.

12. Markus and Kitayama, "Culture and the Self."

13. Eunkook Suh et al., "The Shifting Basis of Life Satisfaction Judgments across Cultures: Emotions versus Norms," *Journal of Personality and Social Psychology* 74, no. 2 (February 1998): 482–93.

14. Roy F. Baumeister, *Identity: Cultural Change and the Struggle for Self* (New York: Oxford University Press, 1986).

15. Oishi, "Psychology of Residential Mobility."

16. Steven J. Heine et al., "Is There a Universal Need for Positive Self-regard?" *Psychological Review* 106, no. 4 (October 1999): 766–94.

17. Jane Gross, "Aging at Home: For a Lucky Few, a Wish Come True," *New York Times*, February 9, 2006, F1, F8.

18. "Facts for Features," U.S. Census Bureau, accessed March 10, 2010, www.census.gov/Press-Release/www/releases/archives/facts_for_features_special_e.

19. Long, "Changing Residence."

20. Frank Oswald and Hans-Werner Wahl, "Dimensions of the Meaning of Home in Later Life: International Perspectives," in *Home and Identity in Late Life*, ed. Graham D. Rowles and Habib Chaudhury (New York: Springer, 2005), 21–45.

21. Robert L. Rubinstein and Patricia A. Parmelee, "Attachment to Place and the Representation of the Life Course by the Elderly," in *Place Attachment*, ed. Irwin Altman and Setha M. Low (New York: Plenum, 1992), 139–63.

22. Edmund Sherman and Joan Dacher, "Cherished Objects and the Home: Their Meaning and Roles in Late Life," in *Home and Identity in Late Life*, ed. Graham D. Rowles and Habib Chaudhury (New York: Springer, 2005), 63–79.

23. Paul G. Surtees et al., "Mastery, Sense of Coherence, and Mortality: Evidence of Independent Associations from the EPIC-Norfolk Prospective Cohort Study," *Health Psychology* 25, no. 1 (January 2006): 102–10; Judith G. Chipperfield and Raymond P. Perry, "Primary- and Secondary-Control Strategies in Later Life: Predicting Hospital Outcomes in Men and Women," *Health Psychology* 25, no. 2 (March 2006): 226–36.

24. Ellen J. Langer and Judith Rodin, "The Effect of Choice and Enhanced Personal Responsibility for the Aged: A Field Experiment in an Institutional Setting," *Journal of Personality and Social Psychology* 34, no. 2 (August 1976): 191–98.

25. Judith Rodin and Ellen J. Langer, "Long-Term Effects of a Control-Relevant Intervention with the Institutionalized Aged," *Journal of Personality and Social Psychology* 35, no. 12 (December 1977): 897–902.

Suggested Readings

Bonner, Barbara, ed. *Sacred Ground: Writing about Home*. Minneapolis, MI: Milkweed, 1996.

Each of the stories and essays in this collection explores the meaning of home and the connection we have with our homes. Writers include Louise Erdrich, Sherman Alexie, and Jim Wayne Miller.

Edwards, John, ed. *Home: The Blueprints of Our Lives*. New York: Harper Collins, 2006.

Fifty-seven Americans from a wide variety of backgrounds describe their childhood homes. The writers include Bob Dole, Steven Spielberg, John Mellencamp, Benicio del Toro, and Vera Wang. The recollections were complied by former senator and vice presidential candidate John Edwards.

Fiffer, Sharon Sloan, and Stever Fiffer, eds. *Home: American Writers Remember Rooms of Their Own*. New York: Vintage, 1995.

Eighteen writers reflect on a home they once knew. The authors include Jane Smiley, Henry Louis Gates Jr., Richard Bausch, and Mona Simpson.

Halpern, Jake. *Braving Home: Dispatches from the Underwater Town, the Lava-Side Inn, and Other Extreme Locales*. Boston: Houghton-Mifflin, 2003.

National Public Radio reporter Jake Halpern visits people who live in places where nature suggests they should not. The common theme among these individuals is the desire to stay in their homes despite constant threats from floods, hurricanes, volcanoes, and the like.

Marcus, Clare Cooper. *House As a Mirror of Self: Exploring the Deeper Meaning of Home*. Berkeley, CA: Conari Press, 1995.

Clare Cooper Marcus, a University of California, Berkeley, architecture professor, uses a Jungian analysis to examine the psychological meaning of home.

Perlman, Mickey, ed. *A Place Called Home: Twenty Writing Women Remember*. New York: St. Martin's, 1996.

Women writers describe a place from their past, most often a home from childhood, and what home means to them. Authors include Erica Jong, Maxine Hong Kingston, Jill McCorkle, and Francine Prose.

Wertsch, Mary Edwards. *Military Brats: Legacies of Childhood inside the Fortress*. New York: Harmony Books, 1991.

Mary Edwards Wertsch, daughter of a career military father, explores some of the consequences of growing up in a military family, including a discussion of the sense of rootlessness that comes from constantly moving during childhood.

Index

About the Author

Jerry M. Burger is professor of psychology at Santa Clara University. He has published dozens of professional articles and chapters and is the author of *Desire for Control: Personality, Social and Clinical Perspectives* and *Personality*, a college-level textbook now in its eighth edition. His research has been featured on *ABC News Primetime*, and he has appeared on *Nightline*, *Anderson Cooper 360*, and *National Public Radio*, among other programs. His work has been described in numerous national and international publications, including *The New York Times*, *USA Today*, *The Washington Post*, *Oprah Magazine*, *Wired*, *Glamour*, *Mademoiselle*, *Vogue*, *Men's Health*, *Ladies Home Journal*, and *Psychology Today*. He and his wife currently live in northern California in the house their son will always think of as his home.